"In *Offshore Angler*, author Mike M catching popular Carolina saltwater game fish in a clear, well-organized fashion. A very experienced angler himself, Marsh instinctively tells the reader the sorts of information anglers need to know to catch fish: what gear you'll need, where to go, what to techniques to try, and how to alter tactics in response to different conditions. If you buy just one book on Carolina offshore angling, this one should be it."—David F. Johnson, Editor, *North Carolina Game & Fish Magazine.*

"In his latest book, *Offshore Angler*, Marsh provides a solid, no-nonsense guide that will be useful for all fishermen, from tyros to seasoned salts, who venture into the waters off the Tar Heel coast. It's a practical, useful book . . . "—Jim Casada, Senior Editor, *Sporting Classics.*

"*Offshore Angler* is one of the most complete guides to catching fish off North Carolina's coast that I've ever read. But one word of warning: Upon finishing this book you could find yourself with an uncontrollable urge to pour lots of money into fiberglass and fishing gear."—Chris Powell, Managing Editor, *Wildlife in North Carolina.*

"*Offshore Angler* is a 'must-read' for any recreational or professional angler. This book contains everything you need or want to know about fishing the North Carolina coast."—Pete Brown, Editor, *Striped Bass Magazine*

"The best part of *Offshore Angler* may be the extensive artificial reef guide. It would be hard to find a more complete guide to our state's artificial reefs . . . ."—Mike Zlotnicki, Outdoors Editor, Raleigh *News & Observer*

"Helpful to any reader—from expert to novice . . . Mike Marsh is among the state's top-five outdoor writers"—Craig Holt, Managing Editor, *North Carolina Sportsman Magazine*

Coastal Carolina Press, Wilmington, NC 28403.
www.coastalcarolinapress.org

First Edition 2004

ISBN 1-928556-44-2

08 07 06 05 04   5 4 3 2 1

Grateful acknowledgement is made to the North Carolina
Department of Marine Fisheries (NCDMF) for permission to
reprint the Artificial Reef Maps, which originally appeared in
North Carolina Artificial Reef Guide, North Carolina Department
of Environment, Health, and Natural Resources, 1995.

Cover & Interior Photographs by Mike Marsh
Book Design by Jane Baldridge/Artspeaks

Printed in the United States.

To Mom

Offshore Angler

Carolina's Mackerel Boat Fishing Guide

Contents

July-September

October-December

Acknowledgments

This book is an organized volume of writings, illustrations and photographs resulting from a combination of knowledge and art. Like most of life's worthwhile endeavors, it is a triumph over pitfalls and hurdles that were overcome through the hard work and dedication of many talented people. I am only the person who gets to sign his name to this book and my thanks go out to everyone else who was on the team that helped to put it together.

Thanks go to the tackle shop owners who helped out with their favorite lures, rigging techniques and fishing hotspots: Jimmy Price and Terry Stewart.

A tip of the fishing cap goes to the sport fishermen and guides who overcame wind, weather, waves and fish that would sometimes not cooperate—and my seemingly endless tinkering with a camera while they were holding fish: David Franklin; Tim Barefoot; John Bobbitt; George O'Neal; Jeff Stokley; Carl Snow, Jr.; Butch Foster; Chris Foster; Dave Dietzler; John Gillilan; David Mammay; Stanley Rudd; Fisher Culbreth; Shawn Ashcroft; Terry Dingler; Joey Hill; Phil Pare; Mike Coleman; Bruce Trujillo; Wayne Freeman; Mark Miller; Jerry Helms; George Beckwith, Jr.; Tom Gore; Ken McGee; and Rick Caton.

Kudos go to the biologists who gave insight into the management and life cycles of fish to help us all conserve them for the future: Eric Gowdy and Dr. Louis Daniel.

Special thanks go to the folks at Coastal Carolina Press and especially my editor, Nikki Smith, for bringing to gaff my many mistakes. Thanks also go to Jane Baldridge of Artspeaks who pulled all the bits and pieces of the puzzle together.

The artificial reef information and maps were provided courtesy of the North Carolina Division of Marine Fisheries (NCDMF). Thanks go to Jim Francesconi of NCDMF who helped out with organizing the artificial reef coordinates, descriptions and maps. Thanks also go to Harry Rolfe who makes Reef Balls for building artificial reefs.

Vic Dunaway deserves high praise for his book, *Sport Fish of the Atlantic*, which helped out with some of the fish descriptions in the glossary.

Most of all, my family needs to know of my deep appreciation for the sacrifices they made. Writing a book is like living with another family member in the house. It needs nurturing and feeding in order to grow. My family sacrificed the enormous amount of time it took me away from them to write this book. They also helped out with the "research" whenever they could get away with me to do some fishing.

watercraft in the event of an emergency at sea. Chemical light sticks and waterproof strobe lights are also important in an emergency situation so that rescuers can find you."

Besides the running lights that are required, a high-powered spotlight is necessary for navigating in the dark. A hand-held, battery-powered light is also essential in the event the boat loses electric power.

A VHF radio is an essential piece of equipment as well, according to Franklin. Cellular phones can also come in handy as backup. But if the angler's out of reach of cellular towers, the radio is his only link to assistance if things go wrong.

"Radios also help anglers find fish," Franklin said. "When fishermen are on the fish, they'll often tell you where they're biting. However, in a tournament situation, they often use code words or are otherwise secretive about where they're fishing. In that case, a radio direction finder can help you pinpoint the places they're fishing but they may not want you to know about. It's sneaky, but not unethical or prohibited and it works."

Two batteries are essential equipment for all offshore boats. Electronics are the lifeblood of a mackerel boat. While one battery may lose power, it's rare to lose both batteries. By using an isolating switch, one battery can be used while the other is rested or saved for an emergency. At times, using both batteries in parallel helps electronic equipment run at peak efficiency.

Franklin also advises twin bilge pumps inside the hull. Even with today's self-bailing hull designs water penetrates into the inner hull through joints, cracks or screw holes in the deck. One pump should be installed with an automatic switch and the other with a manual switch.

"You really can't fish in the ocean without good electronics," Franklin said. "A GPS or Loran unit is necessary for finding structure and navigating to the structure. The Global Positioning System receives its signals from satellites and was intended for military use. The signals were constantly switched for defense purposes, but now they're accurate enough for navigating to within about 100 feet of a position at sea. Loran-C receives its signals from land-based towers and is in the process of being phased out as a navigation aid. Anglers can buy computer programs to convert the Loran-C numbers they've developed over the season into GPS coordinates."

Radar is an expensive item to have aboard a king mackerel boat. However, Franklin believes radar units are the best thing going for safety in poor visibility situations such as haze, fog, thunderstorms and running at night.

"A depthfinder with a recording screen is essential equipment for offshore fishing," Franklin said. "While depth-finding devices can help you navigate or find a good area by telling you the water depth, the recorder will show the fish and the type of bottom cover or structure."

For his personal depthfinder, Franklin likes to use a color machine or "color scope." Sonar units bounce and return signals off the swim bladders of the fish. By indicating the strength of the return signal in color, the color screen tells an experienced angler the types and sizes of fish that are present. The strength of the signal and corresponding color can also tell the angler the hardness of the bottom, indicating sand, coral, rocks or live bottom areas.

"Electronics must be positioned for easy visibility to be effective," Franklin said. "Anglers must also be careful to select models that will be visible in the sunlight. Sometimes screens that look great in the showroom can fade away in bright light."

T-tops are great for storing electronic instrumentation. By keeping electronics in watertight boxes behind the windshield, they're safe from salt spray and easily visible. Electronics can also be mounted on the dash. With cabin boats, electronics mounted on top of the dash are usually protected. However, inside-the-dash mounting also bears consideration where dash space is available because an errant wave washing over the windshield can create havoc with sensitive electronic circuitry.

"No matter how good the electronic navigation equipment aboard, a compass is an essential item of equipment," Franklin said. "If the boat loses electric power, the compass will still work. It also makes it easier to maintain position when fishing a piece of structure and helps orient the boat in a trolling pattern."

Any type of recreational fishing means using rods to catch and land fish. However, offshore fishing requires lots and lots of rods.

"You can't have too many rod holders," Franklin said. "I fish with six rods and have spares onboard. On my boat, we store the rods in a rocket-launcher arrangement on the back of the T-top. When actually fishing, I set out one rod on either side of the T-top and often use an outrigger for each rod that's suspended from the T-top. I set the lines from two rods out on downriggers and set flatlines from two rods off the back corners of the boat.

"Downriggers are essential for catching fish in deep water because sometimes the only strikes will come near the bottom. Downriggers should be situated near the back of the boat, but should still allow the end of the boom to be easily reached. When fishing offshore, wire cable should be used to hold downrigger weights. Wire produces less drag in the water and therefore allows your weight to track deeper. Monofilament is not as durable as steel. Automatic downriggers are nice to have. They can take a lot of work out of cranking in weights and will keep baits down in the strike zone longer because of the speed at which the fishing depth can be controlled."

Livewells are also the key to success at catching many offshore species. Franklin has definite opinions on keeping baits lively.

"The livewell tank should be plastic, not fiberglass," Franklin said. "The tank should also be round. Baitfish species seem to be worn out faster against fiberglass sides. Since they must swim constantly to survive, the round tank prevents them from becoming stuck in corners and smothering."

While Franklin feels a minimum of 30 live baits is necessary for fishing offshore for a day, his livewell tank holds 55 to 60 baits.

"You don't want to put too many baits in a livewell, or they lose their liveliness," Franklin said. "My livewell holds 55 gallons, or about one large menhaden per gallon."

It's important to install the livewell with a freshwater intake and overboard discharge. The inlet should be set at the bottom to flush out fecal matter. The outlet should be at the top to flush out scum.

"A good flow is essential for keeping baits alive," Franklin said. "I use 2,300 gallon-per-hour livewell pumps. Dual pumps, or at least a spare pump, are essential. There's nothing worse than losing a livewell full of bait when a pump quits after reaching a fishing destination offshore."

When everything goes right and a fish is played to the boat, it must be kept fresh for the table. Therefore, consideration must be given to icing the catch.

"I carry two large ice chests filled with ice," Franklin said. "When I catch a fish, I put the fish into the boat's built-in fish storage box. Then I add ice on top of the fish. If you put all the ice into the boat's storage box to start with, you have a difficult time putting lots of big fish into the box because the ice takes up all the space. Back at the dock, you can transfer the fish and ice from the boat's storage box into the coolers for easy transportation."

Selecting the right boat and rigging it out properly are the trademarks of the most successful offshore fishermen. By buying the best boat he can afford and outfitting it with top-of-the line gear and equipment, learning how to use it, and keeping it maintained in top working order, the Offshore Angler will have leaped the first major hurdle in becoming a tournament winner or at catching fish when other anglers fail.

"Knowing where to fish and how to fish are important aspects of a good fishing team and are learned through experience," Franklin said. "But by staying well prepared and using first-class equipment, all offshore anglers can put more fish in their boats."

oceans of the world by 27 percent. There are many theories about the cause of the decline. It could be the result of man-made pollution, or the El Niño and La Niña weather patterns. It could also be the result of atmospheric phenomena such as changes in solar radiation or sunspots, or even changes in ocean temperatures caused by the controversial specter of global warming. However, while the cause of the coral decline is uncertain, its devastating .effect on sea life is unmistakable. Without coral reefs, entire ecosystems disappear and sport-fishing opportunities vanish with along with them.

The advantage of using Reef Balls over traditional artificial reef materials and structures is not only the ease of manufacturing them and transporting them to ocean sites, but in the environmentally-friendly aspects of their manufacturing process. Tankers, train cars, barges, concrete rubble, rubber tires and other cast-offs of modern society must be decontaminated of oils, asbestos, anti-freeze and other sources of pollution prior to being placed in the ocean. Transportation costs, both on land and sea, can also place a prohibitive burden on using "junk" to build artificial reefs.

Reef Balls can be built on small land sites, hauled in small craft to an ocean site and hoisted over the side with a boom and winch. They can even be filled with an inflatable core, floated and towed across the water with small boats. Once at the site, the core is deflated and removed and the Reef Ball sinks.

The Reef Ball manufacturing process is actually quite simple. Concrete is poured into a fiberglass mold. A polyethylene buoy is set in the center of the mold. Various sizes of inflatable plastic balls are placed in the mold to create the openings in the walls. Once the concrete sets, the outer mold is unbolted and the inner buoy is deflated, leaving the characteristic dome shape with multiple entry holes.

While the North Carolina Division of Marine Fisheries (NCDMF) remains scientifically skeptical about the use of Reef Balls in its artificial reef program, it purchased 1,000 of them to add to some of its reefs in 2001. The NCDMF biologists will monitor the sites in an effort to quantify the cost-to-benefit ratio of producing habitat for fish and other bottom life, as well as the increase in recreational opportunities for anglers and divers. NCDMF is monitoring a patch of Reef Balls off the state's central coast in Carteret County and will compare the catch of fish at that location to the catch of fish at more traditional reef types. The agency is not yet committed to the balls, but has taken a definite interest in their design and use.

The Long Bay Reef Association purchased 600 Reef Balls in 2001 and divided them equally among six existing artificial reefs along the southern North Carolina coast. After seeing a dramatic increase in the number and types of species caught at inshore reefs, the association of fishermen and tournament officials didn't need any scientific study to tell them that Reef Balls worked.

The increase in the flounder catch at two reefs that were refurbished with Reef Balls near the mouth of the Cape Fear River created such excitement among fishermen that the Reef Balls were dubbed, "Flounder Hotels." They began attracting fish immediately, without a lengthy waiting period for pioneer plant species to attach themselves to the concrete structures and in turn attract forage fish and predatory fish. Apparently the schooling baitfish found the Reef Balls and immediately began to use their artificial cavities as sanctuaries, attracting fish higher up in the food chain like flounder, which wait outside the Reef Ball "windows" for an easy meal.

On the beach a couple of miles distant from these reefs, the Long Beach Fishing Pier was being rebuilt in the aftermath of Hurricane Floyd. When word of the success of Reef Balls got out, the pier owners decided to drive the pier's new pilings right through Reef Balls to see if they were effective when placed near shore. The 64 Reef Balls surrounding the pier's new pilings quickly resulted in the catch of eight tripletails, a fish rarely caught in North Carolina waters. But the bigger and most significant news was that the Reef Balls also resulted in a 30 percent increase in the pier's catch of flounder.

Chapter 3

Striper Revival

Following one of the snowfalls rare to the North Carolina coast, I received a telephone call from one of the state's top professional guides. Tim Barefoot invited me on a trip to Oregon Inlet to test his new lures. Barefoot operates *No Shoes Charters* out of Wrightsville Beach during the warm months. When the weather turns cold, he heads to North Carolina's northern coast and Oregon Inlet to catch the giant striped bass that have returned to the area after over a decade of protective harvest regulations.

The wind was whistling out of the northwest as we left the ramp at the north side of the inlet. When we turned into the wind after hitting the open Atlantic, the waves were crested with whitecaps. But we braved the waves to head up the beach to a point just offshore from the Bodie Island Lighthouse.

Along for the ride were Barefoot's long-time fishing buddy, John Bobbitt, and George O'Neal of *Tar River Sports*, a wholesale fishing tackle dealership in Greenville that distributes lures of Barefoot's design. Barefoot and Bobbitt are from Wilmington, but they towed Barefoot's catamaran to the northeast coast for a shot at the legendary striped bass run.

Once outside the inlet, Barefoot found evidence of big fish feeding in the water by watching the sky. Thousands of birds were circling and diving into the water. A pelican came up after a power dive with a 2-pound gray trout in its beak and nearly had his breakfast wrestled away by another greedy pelican.

"We're going to use blue-backed *Cha-Raiders* today," Barefoot said. "I call my lures *Cha-Raiders* because they so closely imitate the real baitfish that fish like. These look just like the gray trout the stripers are eating."

Indeed, Barefoot had used a real Boston mackerel and cigar

Captain Tim Barefoot of *No Shoes Charters* and John Bobbitt with a pair of big Oregon Inlet striped bass.

minnow to make the mold for his first lures, but they didn't run true.

"The prototypes didn't swim well, so I trimmed them down until they had the action I liked," Barefoot said. "Now, I have all-purpose lures that can be jigged, cast and retrieved, or trolled. Even at very high speeds, the lures stay stable and run true in the water. When they're jigged, they dart around just like wounded baitfish."

Barefoot was once a mold maker by trade, so he knows the complexities of the plastics manufacturing process. His lures are cast of pure Nylon, with a one-piece wire harness and lead balancing weights. As Barefoot powered down the boat beside a flock of diving birds, Bobbitt made the first cast. A couple of twitches later, he was fighting the first fish of the day.

The fish fought against king mackerel-sized tackle spooled with 50-pound superbraid line for at least 10 minutes before being landed and released. It weighed more than 20 pounds and proved rather smallish when compared to the many fish we were destined to catch the rest of the day.

I cast the hefty weight of a 7-inch *Cha-Raider* into the wind and let the boat drift take the slack out of the line. In seconds, the lure hit the sand beneath 20 feet of water. Jigging the lure in the conventional manner garnered zero attention from the fish, while Bobbitt and O'Neal both hooked up fish.

While they fought their fish, Barefoot coached me in the fine art of *Cha-raider* jigging.

"Cast the lure at an angle to the direction of boat drift and let the lure fall to the bottom," Barefoot said. "When you feel it hit the sand, use a short, fast pull of the rod tip to lift the lure. You can feel it vibrate rapidly as you lift the rod. Feel it through ten or twelve vibrations and let it fall."

After the first pair of stripers were fought to the boat and released, I tested Barefoot's advice and hooked a fish on the next cast. While most fish strike a jigged lure as it falls back down toward the bottom, these fish struck while the lure was swimming toward the surface. With all the slack removed from the line, I could appreciate the full power of a striped bass.

I fought the fish for 15 minutes as it made several runs, refusing to tire against all the drag I cared to apply on 50-pound superbraid line. At the landing net, the duration of the fight was explained. A striper weighing above 40 pounds was a rare fish a decade ago, but my first fish of the day topped that mark.

As Barefoot unhooked the fish, he brought my attention to the leader.

"Some of the trick is in the rigging," he said. "I use an 80-pound, wind-on fluorocarbon leader, which is tough and virtually invisible to the fish. But the key is the knot. I tie the lure to the leader with a loop knot so the knot doesn't impair the side-to-side action of the lure."

For the remainder of the day, we cast, jigged and trolled *Cha-Raiders*. Other boats braved the weather to share in the excellent fishing as well. The fish would sound and seemingly disappear, only to resurface a quarter-mile distant. Our professional spotters, the ever-vigilant sea birds, were always quick to tell us when a feeding school of bass chased baitfish to the surface.

Cha-Raiders are the nearest things to do-everything lures I've seen; Barefoot said he uses them to catch everything that swims. The tough lures may lose a little paint, but are otherwise undamaged by king mackerel, yellowfin tuna, dolphin, stripers, bluefish and other toothy sea monsters. The big chopper bluefish we caught along with the stripers scarcely marred the finish of the lures with their sharp teeth.

Before heading back in, we had hooked and released over 20 fish with many of them weighing more than 30 pounds. They were still biting when we left the area. As Barefoot had promised, we caught them by trolling, casting and jigging his *Cha-Raiders* at all water depths from the top down to the bottom at 25 feet.

Another new lure design Barefoot unveiled was called the *Squid-Sub*. Properly rigging a natural squid so it runs true can take several minutes for an experienced angler. However, Barefoot merely hooked the weighted lure head into the tail of the squid, placed a trailer hook near its head, tossed it over the side and took off. In spite of trolling at an extremely high speed, the squid ran true and didn't wash off until nailed by a fish. According to Barefoot, the depth of the squid is controlled by the length and diameter of the line. Within a hundred feet, the lure snagged a striped bass.

"I love to run charters and help people catch fish," said Barefoot as he played the fish. "That's the main reason I designed my lures. They make catching fish easy for everyone, no matter their experience levels."

We trolled with squid for a couple of miles until we returned to Oregon Inlet. The water was rollicking where the inlet waters ran counter to the wind-waves of the Atlantic. We could see stripers working in the waves, but the water conditions were too dangerous for fishing.

Inside the more sheltered waters in the lee of the beach, striper anglers in small boats were casting jigs and trolling lures near the N.C. Highway 12 Bridge across Oregon Inlet. The ever-circling birds were guiding their success as well. We stopped and bounced a few lures off the bridge pilings to no effect and decided to call it a day. Cold and weary from fighting huge fish in the wind-chopped spray, we were warm on the inside from experiencing the return of the line-sided giants.

Additional Information

Tim Barefoot operates *No Shoes Charters* out of Wrightsville Beach for bottom fish and king mackerel in warm months and for striped bass at Oregon Inlet in winter. *Barefoot Baits* are available at tackle shops. There is also a video that shows the proper knots and leaders to use for rigging *Barefoot Baits.* Call Tim Barefoot at (910) 392-3545 or visit www.barefootbaits.com.

Captain Jimmy Price with a weakfish or "gray trout" caught with a jigging spoon at an artificial reef near Southport.

Chapter 4

Catch Jigger's Wrist From Weakfish and Virginia Mullet

Some anglers think that ocean fishing is lackluster in February and mistakenly stay in the house, watching sports on television until the arrival of warmer weather. These fishermen are missing out on some great light tackle action and fine eating in the form of weakfish and Virginia mullet. Some anglers also call weakfish "gray trout." Fishery managers call them weakfish, so I'll defer to the name weakfish—a name that also tells anglers that the fish have delicate mouths that easily tear free from hooks when too much pressure is applied. Some anglers also call Virginia mullet "whiting."

I checked around local tackle shops and heard that the weakfish had returned to the area. With my son Justin onboard, I headed out on an unusually slick-calm February day to John's Creek, a rock formation a couple of miles south of Masonboro Inlet. The formation extends from Masonboro Island offshore a mile or so, and is marked by the skeletal remains of a maritime forest on Masonboro Island locally known as "The Myrtle Bushes." This forest was defoliated by hurricanes Bertha, Fran, Bonnie, Floyd and Dennis and may one day disappear altogether. Anglers should spot another landmark on the mainland for future reference, or they should mark the spot on their GPS or Loran equipment after finding the ledges on a depthfinder.

Anglers began catching weakfish a few years ago after over a decade of the species being virtually extinct. The weakfish population has been the subject of intense management, including

Weakfish are suckers for jigging spoons, which are manufactured in a variety of styles, sizes and colors.

a reduction in shrimp trawling and flynet fishing in and around Pamlico Sound. According to North Carolina Division of Marine Fisheries statistics, in the recent past, as many as 90 percent of all weakfish were being killed by commercial gear before reaching adulthood. The commercial restrictions and recreational bag and size limits have worked well to restore the fish.

There were several boats taking advantage of the day's spring-like weather to prospect the area for weakfish when Justin and I arrived at our destination. Anglers were using natural baits and lures fished on the bottom. I tied on a 1 1/2-ounce gold *Gibbs Minnow*, which is a jigging and casting spoon with a soft metal body that can be bent to give the lure different types of action. Justin, in his early teens at the time, decided on the lazy option and tied on a standard two-hook bottom rig baited with fresh shrimp. Drifting across the area, it wasn't long before I hooked a fish. Imagine my surprise when Justin netted a Virginia mullet that came to the gunwale instead of a weakfish. Before he set the net down, his rod bent and he began cranking another Virginia mullet onboard. Using binoculars, I scanned other boats and found that everyone was hauling in Virginia mullet.

While a Virginia mullet isn't in the same game fish category with a weakfish because it doesn't fight as well or grow nearly as large, its culinary qualities are second to none. With no bag or size

Virginia Mullet can be caught on small jigging spoons. Some anglers find a school of whiting by using spoons then switch to fresh shrimp.

limit on Virginia mullet, the makings of a fish fry can be caught and kept in short order. In most cases, Virginia mullet are there in large numbers or are completely absent. This was one of the good cases. Within a few minutes, we had enough Virginia mullet for dinner for our family, and enough to invite some friends to join the feast. Most of the fish we caught were hooked in the gills by the jigging spoons—the result of the bottom-feeding position and small size of a Virginia mullet's mouth. They attacked the spoons, but couldn't get their mouths around them. A smaller spoon, in the 3/4-ounce size, resulted in better mouth hook-ups but took much longer to reach the bottom. Most of the Virginia mullet that we caught bit Justin's shrimp offerings.

Satisfied that we had enough Virginia mullets for dinner, we headed for another weakfish honey hole, AR-378, which is 2.6 miles south of Carolina Beach inlet. The reef consists of sunken tires and barges and is marked with a buoy to make it easy to find, even without navigation equipment. There were several boats anchored over the structure, and the fish coming over the boats' gunwales were weakfish.

After hooking and losing several lures on the artificial structure, we drifted inshore off the reef a bit and started catching fish from a deep hole we found by using the depthfinder. We boated eight fish weighing up to 4 pounds in less than 30 minutes—which isn't uncommon when catching weakfish since they're known to stack up in large schools.

Catching a limit of weakfish quickly is great for preventing "jigger's wrist," the fatigue brought on by monotonously twitching the rod up 3 feet and then letting the lure fall back to the bottom. The strikes nearly always occur on the fall, and setting the hook on the slightest hesitation during the fall to the bottom contributes wonderfully to jigger's wrist if the hooks are set into a big weakfish, which can put up a strong fight.

Other lures popular for jigging deep water for weakfish are *Hopkins*, *Silver Bullet*, and *Stingsilver* spoons as well as lead-head jigs. Silver and gold colors give plenty of flash for sunny days, but spoons are also offered in many painted-on colors. Anglers can experiment to see which colors work best on any particular day. I like a wide variety of colors, with red/gold, pink/white and blue/white being some of my favorites.

Weakfish and Virginia mullet are both suckers for fresh shrimp hooked on a bottom rig. Weakfish are also fond of finger-sized, live popeye mullets. Virginia mullet also like bloodworms that can be bought in most bait and tackle shops. Long-shanked No. 2 or No. 4 hooks work well for holding both fish securely.

The best conditions to catch these fish occur on days with calm winds and clear water. The fish have a maddening habit of biting furiously for a short period of time, then stopping completely. Anglers should look for concentrations of fish on the depthfinder, keep their baits and lures working near the bottom and wait for the fish to turn on.

Other places you can catch weakfish and Virginia mullet include: AR-425 off Yaupon Beach, AR-420 off Long Beach and any other near-shore wrecks, ledges and artificial reefs along the coast in waters with depths of up to 40 feet.

When the water turns cold, the sea bass bite gets so hot that anglers like Jeff Stokley catch them three at a time. These were caught at an artificial reef 10 miles off Carolina Beach.

Chapter 5

Have A Blast
Catching Sea Bass

The March wind had been really rollicking for at least a week, keeping all small crafts in port or sitting on trailers in backyards. When a short reprieve from the wind finally came, my neighbor Jeff Stokley, called and asked if I wanted to join him in an attempt to catch some bluefish from his 22-foot boat.

Heading to an area near the erosion-clogged Corncake Inlet just northeast of Bald Head Island, we spotted a school of small blues driving baitfish to the surface beneath a diving school of gulls. Casting gold *Gibbs Minnow* jigging spoons to the bluefish, we caught a few small ones before the fish sounded into the depths. Then the bite shut down for the day.

Stokley explored the area with a depthfinder, circling the rocky bottom to try to find a school of bluefish below the surface. When large shapes on the screen indicated a school of predators feeding on baitfish near the bottom we cast our spoons from the drifting boat.

"Fish on!" Stokley hollered.

The drag on the reel ratcheted slowly against a powerfully-swimming fish that wanted to hug the bottom. We questioned each other—as anglers usually do—about the identity of the fish before it came into view. Was it a sand shark or a skate? Certainly, it didn't possess the speeding streak of a bluefish, we decided. Eventually, the 4 pounds of drag tension on the 10-pound test line urged the mystery fish to the surface.

It was a black sea bass of about 3 pounds. In commercial

jargon, it was jumbo-sized. Honestly hoping the bluefish wouldn't attack our jigging spoons on their way to the bottom we cast, jigged and caught sea bass until our wrists were tired. Since that day, whenever the fickle winds of March relent, we head out for sea bass, confident that they're easy to catch if we head out to any of the ledges and reefs that are so popular among anglers fishing for other species during the summer and fall.

March can be a genuinely boring month for saltwater anglers. Windy days and chilly weather dampen the enthusiasm of the hardiest fishermen. However, there are still fish to be caught when the restless angler tires of tuning his gear and tending to his boat.

One of the best-tasting fish in the sea that's available to anglers on a year-round basis is the black sea bass. It's so common that anglers hook the fish accidentally during trips for other species such as snapper, grouper and weakfish. Because the sea bass' most aggressive schooling of the season occurs in March, they save the day for many restless offshore anglers. It doesn't take much preparation or a long boat ride to catch a limit of fish.

Captain Carl Snow, Jr., of *Fish Witch II Charters* knows a lot about sea bass. Snow operates a 44-foot charter boat out of Carolina Beach and is one of the area's most trusted captains. Like many area charter boat captains, Snow fishes commercially for "blackfish" as black sea bass are called on the docks. When cold weather keeps his regular clients, recreational anglers, at home, sea bass help supplement his income.

"I charter trips for anglers who want to catch sea bass," said Snow. "But during the months of November through March, I also fish blackfish pots. There are lots of really good places to catch sea bass close to shore. On a charter, I probably won't have to go 5 miles out, but I can wind up at the Dredge Wreck about 10 miles from Carolina Beach if necessary to find fish. All of the artificial reefs hold sea bass. The natural reefs and ledges also hold plenty of fish."

According to Snow, sea bass are migratory. Gone by summer and returning when the water cools down, sea bass migrate back into the inshore waters when spring breezes blow.

"Sea bass are very hardy fish," Snow said. "They can withstand a wide range of water temperatures, but seem to like the 56- to 63-degree range the best."

Sea bass are not picky eaters. Snow said that he prefers to use a two-hook bottom rig baited with squid or cut bait to catch these aggressive fish.

"To add some fun, an angler can use a *Hopkins* spoon to jig the reefs and ledges," Snow said. "Catching a big sea bass on light spinning tackle with a spoon can really put a bend in a rod."

Snow, better than most captains, knows a big sea bass when he feels one tug. Through a funding program with North Carolina Sea Grant, he has experimented with growing the fish under laboratory conditions from an 8-inch "pin" into a 2-pound "jumbo" in a matter of 6 to 8 months.

Dr. Wade Watanabe, a research professor at the University of North Carolina at Wilmington's Center for Marine Science, and graduate student Kimberly Copeland helped with the study, which was conducted in tanks at the university's Wrightsville Beach location.

The first part of the project identified which commercial fish diet worked best to help the sea bass put on weight. The second part of the study identified a stocking rate for commercially raised fish. Such aquiculture experiments may someday take the pressure off of wild-caught fish, which are becoming highly managed through quotas and catch limits.

"We shed peeler crabs at our house and want to see if we can raise sea bass in the same environment," Snow said. "Although we can control things like temperature and salinity in the laboratory, we don't know if we can raise sea bass under real world conditions. Wade Watanabe knows his stuff. He has actually spawned sea bass in the laboratory, so we hope we can raise the fish successfully."

Special regulations are scheduled for anglers who want to catch sea bass north of Cape Hatteras, according to Dr. Louis

Robert Connelly shows that sea bass are great for introducing kids to saltwater fishing.

Daniel of the North Carolina Division of Marine Fisheries (NCDMF).

"We have two stocks of fish that will now be subject to two different sets of regulations," Daniel said. "We find that the two stocks tend to migrate inshore and offshore rather than from north to south with the temperature changes. Therefore the two stocks are managed under separate regulatory bodies. The stock north of Cape Hatteras is under pressure from fishermen in northern states."

Recreational fishing regulations for sea bass under the new, two-zone system were adopted at a council meeting in January 2001 and have been implemented in the years since. North Carolina anglers fishing north and south of Cape Hatteras should check with NCDMF before heading out for sea bass since the waters will probably continue to have different regulations for some time.

Other regulations aimed at increasing sea bass numbers include requiring cull rings and escapement doors in pots to eliminate concerns with "ghost pots," which are lost or abandoned traps that keep catching and killing fish. All this adds up to an increase in fish available to southern coastal anglers.

Eric Gowdy, a technician who works for NCDMF in Wrightsville Beach, likes catching sea bass from the nearby reefs.

"We use chum to bring them up to the surface," Gowdy said. "Sometimes when they come up, they're so plentiful you could scoop them up in a landing net."

Gowdy uses frozen squid or commercial chum to concentrate sea bass. Once he spots the fish, he casts to them with a jig or cut bait on light spinning tackle—but sometimes the fish aren't located directly on the structure. At times they only swim near the structure.

"We spot the fish with a depthfinder or color scope," Gowdy said. "Sometimes they're right on the bottom and at other times, they move right on up to within 10 feet of the surface. The more actively they're feeding, the more likely they are to be moving away from the structure."

Like Snow, Gowdy said sea bass can be caught anywhere there's hard structure.

"Any of the ledges that hold grouper and snapper are great for catching sea bass when they're offshore," Gowdy said. "When they're in close early in the year, I find them at places like Ten-mile Rock, the Wrightsville Beach Reef, and Five-mile Boxcars. The Five-mile Boxcars reef has a natural ledge nearby that holds lots of big sea bass that can really put up a fight. When the fish are deep and right on the structure, I like to use squid as bait. There are lots of other fish besides small sea bass on the reefs and ledges that can nibble on a bait. The advantage of squid is durability. It stays on the hook a long time and tends to catch more sea bass than other baits. I like to use a two-hook bottom rig with a 3-ounce or 4-ounce bank sinker to catch them on the ledges."

The best reason to target sea bass in March is because there are fewer bait-stealers around than in the warmer months. Catching a limit of sea bass without spending a lot on bait becomes a much more likely proposition. Many anglers jigging for weakfish on the natural ledges just off Fort Fisher—like Sheephead Rock and High Rock, as well as Lighthouse Rock in the Cape Fear River mouth—keep coming up with jumbo-sized black sea bass in March and April when even the weakfish have lockjaw. Sea bass can be caught just like gray trout, by using *Gibb's*, *Stingsilver*, *Hopkins*, and *Mega Bait* jigging spoons. The old standby *Diamond Jig* is also a popular lure.

The trick when using jigging spoons is to let the lure fall to the bottom, then quickly reel it up 2 to 4 feet. The lure is jigged just above the bottom to attract a strike. Sea bass will be attracted to the lure by sight from several feet away. Finding hard structure in clear water is the key to jigging success. When the water is cloudy, it's more productive to use cut bait.

Additional Information

Captain Carl Snow, Jr. operates *Fish Witch II Charters* out of Carolina Beach and specializes in all types of inshore and offshore fishing.

Anglers can reach Snow by calling (910) 458-5155.

Chapter 6

Unlocking Spanish Mackerel Secrets

There's nothing that quickens an angler's pulse like tasting salt spray as he cuts through the final breaker of an inlet toward the reddening face of dawn—except perhaps the anticipation of catching an ice chest full of feisty fish in short order. A flock of birds diving into a school of baitfish just beyond the beaches can give the angler a clue that Spanish mackerel are lurking below, luring him within casting or trolling range.

While some anglers are wildly successful at catching limits of this highly prized game and food fish, others spend the day chasing schools with only an occasional strike. There's no doubt that Spanish mackerel can be finicky feeders, and it's the angler with a wide range of tactics and tackle aboard who will have the greatest success on a consistent basis.

Finding fish is the first order of business for the Spanish mackerel angler. The best thing to do before heading offshore is to ask operators of local tackle shops, marinas and fellow fishermen where the fish have been showing up near the surface. The fish are fairly reliable and frequent the same areas from day to day, so heading out to those places helps conserve fishing time. If an angler heads to a likely location and sees boats trolling the area without much luck, switching on a VHF radio is a quick way to find other hot spots. Anglers are usually willing to provide information over the airwaves about where to find Spanish mackerel.

The first thing to find is a flock of small birds diving toward

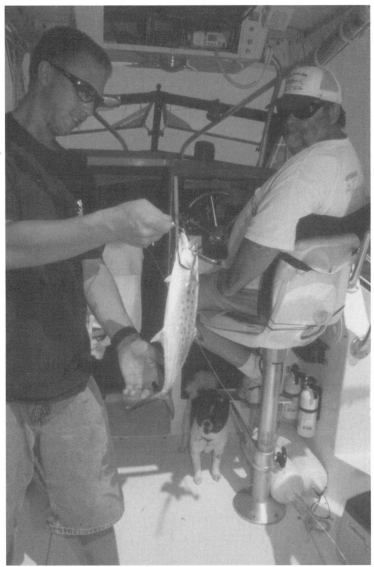

Captain Butch Foster of *Yeah Right Charters* in Southport and his son and mate, Chris, catch lots of Spanish mackerel at artificial reefs by trolling spoons.

the surface. Pelicans are not reliable indicators of feeding Spanish mackerel because they eat large baitfish. It's the smaller skimmers, terns and seagulls that tip off anglers to the presence of Spanish mackerel. These birds can see far down into the water. Even if they're only circling and not actively diving, they may be waiting for finny predators to chase schools of baitfish out of the depths and to the surface.

The next best clue is the presence of other boats. Boats often congregate around schools of Spanish mackerel. The popular tactic of trolling often creates trolling circles or alleys, where boats traveling in the same direction give away the locations of schools. Finding an opening and joining the merry-go-round can quickly get anglers in on the fun.

Certain conditions can cause the fish to go deep. Heat, cold, rain, wind and a bright overhead sun can send Spanish mackerel to the depths. An electronic depthfinder will show an angler how deep to jig or troll to catch the fish.

Trolling with spoons is the most popular way of catching Spanish mackerel. Most anglers find that the fish prefer silver spoons for bright days and gold spoons on overcast days. The size of the spoon can be an important factor in catching fish. Most often, spoons in sizes No. 1 or No. 0 are very effective. But when the fish are finicky, moving down to size No. 00 can turn them on.

It pays to watch the surface to see what size of baitfish the Spanish are feeding on.

Another clue is examining the inside of an ice chest after placing a fish inside. Spanish eject the contents of their stomachs when caught and the angler should try to match the size of his lure to the size of the ejected baitfish.

Leaders deserve special consideration. Typically, anglers begin by using 30-pound test mono leaders 15 feet in length. However, the fish are notoriously shy of leaders and lengthening them, decreasing the diameter or switching back and forth between different-colored leaders can increase strikes.

The use of trolling weights and planers to take spoons below the surface is part of the trolling game. Anglers who want to consistently catch fish must be familiar with this gear. Even while part of a school is feeding on the surface, other members of the same school are far down below. A typical four-rod spread for trolling includes a pair of surface lines with no weight ahead of the spoons, or with small trolling weights, plus two rods equipped with No. 3, 2, 1 or 0 planers.

Planers allow a lure to be trolled as deep as 30 feet beneath the surface and are often the only choice for trolling in the middle of the day when light penetration sends the fish deep. Some anglers skip using rods altogether when using planers and use hand lines instead. Planers are metal or plastic diving planes that take the lure down to the fish by providing an angled profile with resistance against the direction of travel when set. Planers "trip," or expose their edges to the direction of travel, and thereby decrease their resistance when a fish strikes the lure. When planers trip they bring small fish like Spanish mackerel up to the surface.

No matter what spoon and diving weight combination you prefer, it's advisable to wear gloves and use long leaders when landing Spanish. The best tactic is to grab the leader as it approaches the rod tip, hand line the fish aboard and swing it directly into an open cooler. Pull the fish to a corner of cooler and hold it in place with the lid, making sure that only the spoon and the fish's jaw are protruding. You can work the spoon free without the fish's tiny scales gluing themselves to your hands and the boat deck. This method also protects you from the Spanish's razor-sharp teeth and prevents the fish from spewing its stomach contents all over the boat deck.

Trolling the edge of a school is more productive than running a boat through the fish. Too much commotion drives the fish deep or scatters the school. The best tactic is to troll in the same direction, and slightly off to one side, of the moving school. Circling the school may cut them off and send them deep. Trolling behind the school results in fewer strikes because the fish are facing the opposite direction.

Some anglers find schools of Spanish mackerel when they're searching for other fish and have no trolling gear, or they just prefer to catch them by casting. Baitcasting tackle and spinning tackle are both good choices for catching Spanish mackerel and can be a lot more fun than trolling gear.

Once a school is spotted feeding at the surface, the boat is eased within casting range. The thin metal spoons popular for trolling don't make the best lures for casting. Heavier casting spoons, jigging spoons, hair jigs, tinsel jigs, metal tube jerk baits, surface popping lures and minnow-imitating plugs all entice Spanish mackerel to strike. The best lures cast a long distance, even in a breeze, have lots of reflective capacity and work best when retrieved at a fast pace.

Casting spoons are ideal lures in all these respects. They're very compact and designed for fast retrieves. Metal-color finishes act like mirrors to catch the sun's rays and they have the added advantage of being constructed of materials that endure constant abuse from sharp teeth. Short lengths of wire or heavy mono leader are necessary when casting lures for Spanish mackerel or the lures can be cut off.

Metal tube lures come in colors like gold, silver, red and white, orange and white and chartreuse and white. These easy-to-cast lures can be trolled, cast, jigged or allowed to sink as far as the angler desires before being retrieved. The forward dip in the "chin" of the lure helps it to dig deep into the water, making it one of the best for casting to visible fish.

Jigs or jigging spoons work well in the middle of the day when the fish are deep. They also work best when the fish are suspended around artificial or natural reefs.

Once a Spanish mackerel is hooked, its attempts to escape will attract other fish right up to the side of the boat. Other anglers casting near the hooked fish will often experience hook-ups.

Saltwater fly fishermen nearly always cut their teeth on Spanish mackerel because they're the perfect targets for fly-fishing gear. Easy to spot and seldom spooked by a fly line, Spanish mackerel readily take flies.

Resin-bodied flies and saltwater flies tied with artificial dressings are good choices because of their durability. Floating fly

Captain Dave Dietzler of *Cape Lookout Charters* in Morehead City catches super-sized Spanish mackerel by using live baits cast on light tackle.

lines work fine for surface-feeding fish, which is a real benefit to a fly angler. Floating lines are the easiest type to use when picking up a fly while preparing to make a repeat cast.

For the largest Spanish mackerel, many anglers prefer to use live bait. Menhaden of about 4 inches in length are the preferred bait for this type of fishing, and their large size keeps the smaller fish from striking them. Trophy-sized Spanish weighing up to 5 pounds can be found schooling around artificial reefs. The bait is presented on a single treble hook with one barb inserted into the nostrils, or at the dorsal or anal fin. The bait is then allowed to swim without any weight on a line without tension to make it appear as natural as possible. This tactic is known as "light lining."

Captain Dave Dietzler of Morehead City specializes in catching trophy-sized Spanish mackerel near the inlets instead of at the artificial reefs. He fishes downstream of the sandbars during falling tide stages and casts live baits into schools of leaping fish. He uses live mullets about 6 inches in length and hooks them with a single treble hook through the nose.

"It's easy to catch limits of small Spanish by trolling with heavy rods and reels," Dietzler said. "But catching a 4-pound Spanish on light spinning gear is what really turns it into a sport-fishing proposition. You get to see the fish when they strike and they're strong fighters. They can strip off a hundred yards of line before you can turn them around and they're also great to eat. What more can anyone ask of a game fish?"

Additional Information

Captain Dave Dietzler operates *Cape Lookout Charters* out of Morehead City. Anglers can contact him at (910) 252-240-2850.

Captain Butch Foster operates *Yeah Right Charters* out of Southport. Anglers can contact him at (910) 845-2004.

John Gillilan caught his cobia from a coral bottom area 30 miles off the beach.

Chapter 7

Championship Wrestling With Cobia

Cobia are the championship wrestlers of offshore saltwater fishing. Big, bad, ugly and mean, these saltwater heavyweights don't display aerial acrobatics, lightning-fast runs or spectacular colors. They just slug it out with an angler in a piscatorial wrestling match. For the unprepared or unwise, these fish can tear up tackle, straighten gaffs, shatter ice chests and create havoc in a cockpit. It's a good thing King Neptune didn't think it was a good idea to equip these back-alley brawlers with a hefty set of dentures; they'd probably eat the boat if you brought them aboard without sufficiently wearing them down or "playing" them at the end of a fishing line.

The beautiful thing about cobia for anglers who've waited since the previous fall to gird for battle with a big boy is that the fish show up in their strongest numbers during the merry month of May, and their earliest showing in the state is off the beaches of the southeastern coast. Cobia are usually caught by anglers who troll with live baits or frozen baits while trying to catch king mackerel.

Catching a cobia on a typical king mackerel bait, terminal rig and rod and reel is what gives the fish its well-deserved reputation. Twenty-pound class tackle is ultra light gear for catching a fish as strong and large as a cobia, which can routinely weigh above 40 pounds. The typical king mackerel rig is tied with tiny No. 3 to No. 5 single-strand wire. If a cobia is hooked on such light tackle, the angler must play a waiting game to successfully land the fish. A short fight with an average-sized cobia takes about 45 minutes on king mackerel tackle. Some anglers try to hurry the match and tighten the drag. But that's a big mistake with a fish as big and powerful as a cobia. The leader breaks or the hooks straighten, resulting in a lost fish.

I once fished with an impatient captain who complained the entire time the rest of the crew fought their cobia on king mackerel tackle. Three anglers in succession boated cobia while he shouted, "Hurry up and get him in!" He was more interested in continuing his trolling than catching the cobia. But, eventually, it was his turn on the rod. I timed him with a watch while maneuvering the boat during the battle. Sure enough, it took him nearly an hour to boat his fish, just like all of the other anglers. Catching four cobia used up much of the fishing day. But with the culinary attributes of cobia, we were happy to have them in the box instead of king mackerel, and even the captain was glad we didn't strain the gear and risk losing any of the huge fish.

To specifically target cobia, most anglers use heavy tackle to catch the fish. Going with a rod that has a heavier action than a typical live bait king mackerel rod is a good idea. Spooling the reel with at least 30-pound test mono is another. When trolling for Cobia, I use No. 7 wire leader and No. 2 treble hooks. Cobia are not nearly as leader shy as king mackerel, so switching to the heavier terminal tackle works well because it allows the angler to use heavier drag tension at the reel to tire the fish, without risking pulled hooks.

Cobia like to "ball" the bait when they strike and can wrap the leader with their tails as they encircle it with their bodies. Using a wire leader of at least 3 feet in length will help to boat the fish. A typical cobia has leader marks on its head, body and tail when it's boated. A cobia's skin won't abrade the leader, but if the leader's test weight is too light and wraps around the fish, he can easily break the leader with his body contortions during a battle.

Cobia are opportunistic feeders. They can be caught on cut fish, live fish, dead fish, crabs, eels and lures that imitate these baits. While slow-trolling or bottom fishing for cobia, it's a good idea to have a heavy spinning rod handy rigged with a natural bait, a large jig or floating popper for sight-casting if a fish shows up at the surface. Cobia are attracted to floating structure and often show up beneath a boat when looking for shade. They also run in schools of two to six fish. Hooked fish often bring the other fish along as they near the boat, and a double or triple hook-up can be made if anglers are ready to present additional baits and lures.

Slow-trolled baits should be presented in a variety of ways because cobia can be persnickety at times. A cobia will follow along behind a bait, sniff it, then fade away like a submerging submarine if he doesn't like what he sees or smells. It's a good idea to have some baits rigged with skirts, some "naked" and some perfumed with saltwater scent. Personally, I like flashy skirts like dolphin-colored Mylar. I think the yellow-green flash draws the fish to the spread and if a cobia doesn't like that particular bait he'll at least choose another from the buffet. In my opinion, scent is the most important thing to use to dress up a cobia bait. I've seldom seen the sniff-and-submerge routine with scented bait. The fish just eats the bait, the reel's warning clicker initiates the action like a ringside bell and the wrestling match is on.

When soaking a bait on the bottom for cobia, some anglers use whole blue crabs to prevent other fish like bluefish and pinfish from eating the bait. They also switch to a large single hook of 7/0 and up, and may even go up to 50-pound test line and 100-pound mono leader. Suspending a single bait just off the top of a wreck or artificial reef and additional baits at different levels down to the bottom covers all the bases. If a cobia's around, he'll find one of the baits rather quickly, so anglers should be prepared for the strike when dropping any bait.

Anytime an angler fishes a wreck or reef identified with a floating marker buoy, he should investigate the buoy. Cobia are notorious for hiding nearby. A pair of polarized sunglasses will help you spot fish in the shadow of a buoy. Even if there's not a cobia in sight, suspending a bait near a buoy or slow-trolling around it is one of the best ways to catch a fish.

Once hooked near any structure, cobia can strip line in a hurry, wrap it and cut it off. The best way to maneuver a fish away from a buoy cable, jetty or wreck is to keep steady pressure on, with as much drag as the tackle can withstand, by driving the boat away at a perpendicular angle. Cobia will make one long run, then one or two shorter runs. Most of the battle will then be fought within sight of the boat, with the fish pumped time after time tantalizingly close to the gaff, then sounding to the bottom and resurfacing 30 yards away.

Buoys, piers, jetties, reefs and wrecks all have cobia swimming near them in May. The Wrightsville Beach jetties, all the inlet sea buoys and the Cape Fear River channel buoys, AR-355, 360, 370, 372, 376, 378, 382, 386, 425 and 420 are all good places to catch a cobia. Even anglers trolling the open water will see them swimming behind the boat. All anyone has to do to land a cobia is be prepared to hook it when the opportunity is presented, then be patient while fighting the fish.

Chapter 8

Fast Action King Mackerel With Live Baits

It could have been one of those early dawns, with the sunrise yawning and winking pink, creating a kaleidoscope vision among the clouds above the rippled Atlantic as the boat sliced through the rollers of an inlet. But it wasn't.

Instead we were stuck idling inside the mouth of a coastal river, watching the brown pelicans circle and descend. Graceful in flight, they clumsily splashed into the water, pouched bills ballooning open. Once in a while one of them caught a menhaden as evidenced by a gulp and bulging throat once the bird had surfaced and strained the gallon of water from his catch through the gap between his upper and lower bill.

Like these feathered fishermen, we had also been chasing baitfish for an hour with scant luck. My Southport guide was David Mammay. He watched a depthfinder screen intently, trying to find the location of the elusive baitfish.

"There they are," he shouted.

Running to the bow, he gathered up his cast net and spread it across a 20-foot diameter circle of water. This time, unlike the several dozen previous casts, the net did not sink to the bottom. The mass of "pogies" swimming in the net buoyed it to the surface. Mammay needed my help to haul the net and its catch of menhaden into the boat.

As we culled injured fish over the stern while tossing many of the flipping silver baits into the boat's livewell, the hungry pelicans gathered to share our good fortune. Baited up, we blasted off, heading out into the ocean through the river mouth with the sun high and bright on our faces.

When slow-trolling live baits for king mackerel during tournaments, getting an early start means catching bait quickly, sometimes in the dark. "First catch bait, then go fishing" is the rule of the successful live bait angler. However, a 40-pound smoker king can strike a live bait at any time of day, so the time it takes to catch the perfect bait must never be considered "wasted" fishing time, although sometimes the chase for bait can knock hours off an offshore fishing foray.

It was five minutes before 10 o'clock when we finished setting out a spread of live menhaden to troll at idle speed behind the boat. It still wasn't yet 10 o'clock when the boat passed the buoy that marked the Yaupon artificial reef and the first king skyrocketed from the water like a Polaris missile. While he was in the air, all reels were silent. But when he crashed back down, a flatline clip snapped, a reel whined. Picking up the rod, I delicately played the fish to the boat while Mammay reeled in the rest of the lines to clear the fight area. Thirty minutes later, he slipped the gaff into a 30-pound king mackerel.

For the rest of the day, we couldn't get a complete spread of baits into the water. Sometimes we would finish setting out the pair of rods known as flatlines, with baits set so close inside the prop wash that the lines from the rod tips were release-clipped to the transom to keep the baits in the water, without a strike. If we did manage to finish setting the flatlines, a fish would often hit the first bait set out from a downrigger, or one of the longer "shotgun" lines as it was being set out. But never again did we get all six baits—two long lines, two flatlines and two downrigger lines—in the water before it was again pandemonium in the cockpit. We soon caught a limit of big kingfish.

Such adventures are not at all rare along the Carolina coast. By midsummer, king mackerel are everywhere there's ocean water, from inlet mouths to the Gulf Stream. While many king mackerel are caught using frozen baits and artificial lures, using live baits is

Slow-trolling with live menhaden accounts for more big king mackerel than any other method.

the most effective way to catch a limit of big kings.

Most anglers use large menhaden for king bait. Knowing how to spread a 7 to 12-foot radius cast net efficiently is a sure way to be asked to become part of the crew on a king mackerel fishing trip. These nets can weigh 30 pounds and practicing on a picnic table in the backyard is the best way to be sure of a making a perfect cast onto the telltale surface "flip" of a menhaden from a rocking boat bow.

Sometimes, menhaden are scarce and mullet are substituted as baitfish. But many anglers overlook other alternative baits. I have successfully used spots, croakers, pinfish and sea bass, which can be caught on hook-and-line when schooling baitfish are scarce. Trimming off the stiff dorsal and pectoral fins of alternative baits with a pair of scissors prevents them from twisting the line. Other good live baits like cigar minnows can be caught offshore on gold-hook rigs with luminescent beads and feathers.

Baits are kept alive inside a livewell. Most expert anglers agree that a ratio of one large menhaden per gallon of water volume in the livewell tank is a good rule of thumb that will keep baits frisky until mid-afternoon. More baits can be added to the livewell on shorter trips and fewer baits on trips that last from sunup to sundown. Pumping systems that bring in freshwater and discharge the "used" water over the side are standard on king mackerel boats. Since menhaden and mullets are filter feeders, they will starve or suffer from oxygen depravation inside a re-circulating system.

The terminal rig is the most important aspect of live-bait fishing for king mackerel. In general, the lighter and more invisible the rig, the better the odds of inducing a strike and, conversely, the better the odds of losing a fish.

The basic Carolina king mackerel rig as tied by Mammay consists of a pair of No. 4x treble hooks spaced 5 inches apart on a wire leader. The front hook holds the bait through the nostrils, the roof of the mouth or behind the head. The back hook is set into the fish near the dorsal or anal fin or allowed to trail freely. The rig can be fished "naked" or dressed up by adding a colored skirt or beads ahead of the bait.

Leaders must be made with wire, or a king will bite through them. Most anglers use leaders that extend 3 feet above the nose hook. Plastic coated or uncoated seven-strand wire can be used, with figure-8 knots securing hooks. However, most anglers prefer single-strand wire, using five barrel wraps and a haywire twist to secure the hooks.

Currently, fluorocarbon is the rage because of its invisibility and durability. Substituted for the front 2 feet of the wire leader, it is secured to the remaining 1 foot by using an *Albright* knot. Titanium wire has recently become available. Because it has a smaller diameter than stainless steel wire of the same test weight it's making a splash among tournament professionals. There's also a coated steel, multi-stranded *Tyger* wire leader material that can be tied using monofilament knots.

"I use single-strand wire for most of my charter trips," Mammay said. "In most cases, it does the trick. When the fish are being finicky and I just have to get one for my anglers, I use the fluorocarbon leader. It's very expensive to tie, much more so than using an all-steel leader. Another time to go to the fluorocarbon is during a tournament when there's a lot of money at stake."

Anglers must always watch for new innovations in leader materials because making the leader invisible and durable are the keys to drawing strikes from the largest kings. In the old days we made up our own rigs. Today, you can find good rigs in tackle shops. All are tied to the line by using a swivel.

Leaders can vary in weight from No. 7 to No. 3, or about 80-pound to 20-pound test. Hooks can vary in size from No. 6x to No. 2x and can be used in multiples greater than two, especially when using long baits like mullet and ribbonfish. The lighter the leader, the more skill anglers must have to boat a big fish.

Rods for live-bait fishing run on the light side as well. Limber rods of around 7 feet in length are preferred because they have the flexibility to allow the bait to be presented as naturally as possible. Heavy action rods tend to pull and jerk the bait in rhythm to the wave action, putting too much strain on the baits. Preferred line classes range from 20 to 40 pounds, although some professionals use lighter lines to induce more strikes from wary large kings. While heavier lines have some abrasion resistance, any nick in the smaller lines will result in lost fish. Innovations in lines are constant. King mackerel anglers should always be on the lookout for smaller, less visible and more abrasion-resistant lines.

Fortunately for skilled anglers, large lines are not needed to bring even the biggest king mackerel to the boat. Most anglers use drag settings of 3 to 5 pounds. Heavier drag settings will likely result in the hooks pulling free or leaders parting rather than a snapped line. Drags must be silky smooth, or the initial break-neck run of a king mackerel will cause the hooks to pull free. Novices must also be admonished against "setting the hook," which really means, "pulling the hook free," when using such light tackle. King

Captain David Mammay with a big king mackerel caught with a live menhaden.

mackerel hook themselves on live-bait rigs. The rod is merely picked up and the line kept taut when the fish makes its first run.

"With a king mackerel, the battle is more akin to fighting a trout with a fly rod than a tug-o-war," Mammay said. "Finesse and patience are the keys to catching a 40-pound king. A battle with a smoker can take as long as 45 minutes, while a snake quickly tires and comes to the boat. On light tackle, one minute of fight per pound of fish is the general rule."

Once the fish is near the gunwale, the tension mounts. When the line grows short, the pull on the hook set is greater and the hooks can fly free. Top anglers use extremely long gaffs to boat kings. It's important for the gaff point to stay well behind the hooks when gaffing a king mackerel. With the point facing downward, the gaff is simply brought into contact with the back of the fish and smoothly pulled toward the angler. The fish is then brought aboard in a single motion.

Finding concentrations of king mackerel is fairly easy. Nautical charts show the locations of natural and artificial reefs. Pier reports tell anglers when kings are right on the beaches. Charts, compasses, Loran and GPS navigation equipment, electronic depthfinders and color scopes, and VHF radios to stay in contact with other anglers are all necessary equipment when it comes to successfully locating kings.

To pursue kings on a regular basis out to 30 miles takes a center console boat of 24 to 30 feet in length. Many of these sleek fishing machines are capable of speeds exceeding 60 miles-per-hour, yet slow to inch-along speed for slow-trolling live baits. They are also expensive to buy and maintain. To the dyed-in-the-brine angler, there's nothing like hearing a reel scream "Fish on!" to justify the time, effort and cost of catching the number one offshore big game fish of the Carolina coast.

Mammay moved from Southport to Alaska, but said he may return to coastal North Carolina during 2004. He didn't know whether he would return to charter boat fishing under his former boat name, *Reel Success*.

King Mackerel Mercury Advisory

In March of 2000, North Carolina, South Carolina, Georgia and Florida issued a joint health advisory concerning high levels of mercury in large king mackerel. The states' health officials said that king mackerel less than 33 inches fork-length (from the nose to the fork of the tail) are safe to eat, but that king mackerel over 39 inches shouldn't be eaten. People should also limit their consumption of fish between 33 and 39 inches. Women of child-bearing age and children age 12 and younger should eat no more than one 8-ounce portion per month, and other adults should eat no more than four 8-ounce portions per month.

Mercury has been shown to cause brain damage in children and unborn babies. The North Carolina Division of Marine Fisheries (NCDMF) tested many king mackerel mercury levels during 1998-99. The findings resulted in the mercury advisory.

"We collected a wide range of king mackerel from both commercial and recreational fisheries," said Dr. Louis Daniel, of NCDMF. "The findings were consistent. Large king mackerel contained high levels of mercury. But fish don't know state boundaries. The king mackerel population off of North Carolina's coast ranges to Florida."

Mercury in fish is an international problem and occurs in freshwater as well as saltwater, urbanized areas as well as wilderness areas. While its source is not conclusively known, airborne pollution from industrial sources like coal-burning industries, chlorine manufacturing facilities and waste incinerators are suspected. It could also be that mercury occurs naturally in high concentrations, but scientists have only recently begun to test for mercury in some fish. Mercury passes up the food chain and concentrates in predatory fish. That's why younger, smaller fish have lower concentrations of mercury than older, larger fish.

Chapter 9

Get the Lowdown on Grouper and Other Bottom Fish

There are many species of reef fish that anglers commonly call "bottom fish." Sea bass, triggerfish, porgies, grunts, snappers and groupers are routinely sought and caught by anglers who fish the deeper ledges and coral bottoms off the Carolina coast. But if you ask any recreational angler what fish he's targeting when heading offshore for a day of bottom fishing, he'll invariably answer, "Grouper."

The grouper is the big game of bottom fishing. Grouper weighing more than 20 pounds are not a rare catch, and the world records for most of the grouper species found in waters off the coast of North Carolina are in the 40- to 50-pound range. Therefore, anglers use heavy tackle when bottom fishing. Serious grouper anglers select lines of 50-pound test and higher with heavy rods and reels suited to this line class. Grouper are strong fighters and like to head for caves and crevasses in rock and coral formations when hooked, and the battle is often won or lost in the instant after the hook is set. If the angler doesn't get the fish turned toward the surface immediately and the fish makes it into a hole or beneath overhanging structure, the result is nearly always a snapped line.

Grouper tackle serves well for all other bottom fish species. When smaller fish are hooked, they're merely winched to the surface. Most of the snappers caught by recreational anglers, for example, weigh less than 10 pounds. While some species of snapper can exceed 20 pounds in waters off the Carolinas they still

Stanley Rudd caught this big red grouper near an offshore wreck.

don't have the strength of large grouper.

Most bottom fish species are subject to size and creel limits. Some species, like the huge Jewfish (recently renamed the Goliath grouper) and the Nassau grouper that can weigh hundreds of pounds, are totally protected because they're quite rare. Beginning anglers should have an identification book or chart on board, or should fish with experienced fishermen until they're familiar with which species they're catching, along with the legal numbers and sizes. These fish go by so many common and local names that merely asking what the legal limits are at a tackle shop or on the docks doesn't guarantee an accurate answer. Anglers must do their homework before bottom fishing.

One of my fishing buddies is a recreational angler who enjoys catching grouper. He fishes aboard his boat, *Little Bit*, and likes to run to marker WR4 at the wreck of the *John Gill* when the bottom fish are inshore of the Gulf Stream.

Rudd also does some high-speed surface trolling in the area. However, on calm days, he often anchors over one of the many ledges for which the area is famous and catches bottom fish like grouper, snapper, triggerfish and black sea bass.

"If trolling is slow or if I have kids onboard, I like to try for grouper," Rudd said. "It gives a nice break from trolling, saves fuel and everyone likes to eat fresh grouper fillets."

Rudd keeps grouper bait frozen on ice. By keeping bait frozen, it can be thawed as needed and any bait not used can be replaced in the freezer back at home after a day of fishing. Squid, cigar minnows and chub minnows are good bottom fish baits.

Rudd uses both electric reels and manual reels in 4/0 and 6/0 sizes. Spooled with 50 or 60-pound test monofilament line, even his pool-cue-sized rods aren't enough to winch big grouper from caves and crevasses in the rocky ledges at times. To some anglers, manual reels provide more sport than electric reels. However, electric reels bring rigs back to the surface quickly and turn the tide of battle in favor of the angler when a big grouper must be hauled away from jagged bottom structure to avoid a cut line. At

Catching a triggerfish during a bottom fishing trip means great eating back "on the hill."

the end of the day, anglers who use electric reels will have dropped and retrieved more baits and reeled in more fish with less effort than anglers using manual reels.

"You have to be quick, and set the hook at the slightest tug on the bait," Rudd said. "Otherwise the fish will get into the rocks and you'll lose the rig and the fish."

His rig is a standard, double-hook bottom rig with up to 1 pound of weight. Circle hooks of 7/0 to 11/0 size are preferred because they hold the fish securely on the trip to the boat from the bottom. The rig is tied with 150-pound test monofilament. The sinker is the bank sinker type, which has a teardrop shape to keep hang-ups to a minimum. Sinkers may have to be heavier or lighter than 1 pound depending upon conditions. The key is using just enough weight to carry the bait to the bottom quickly and still allow a good "feel" for the bottom based on water depth and sea conditions.

"Using two hooks can increase the catch," Rudd said. "When there are plenty of fish, double hook-ups aren't uncommon. You can also offer two baits on a two-hook rig. We often catch small reef fish like cigar minnows and tomtates on the ledges by using a *Sabiki* rig, which is a rig tied with multiple gold hooks dressed with luminous beads and feathers. When you cut these fresh baits and frozen baits into chunks and offer a smorgasbord, you never know what you're going to reel in next."

The main trick for successful bottom fishing is the use of electronic equipment. Ledges and reefs that hold fish are found by using sonar equipment. Once a productive ledge is located, it can be logged into the memory of a Loran or GPS unit for future reference.

Establishing the anchor coarse is often the toughest part of bottom fishing. The combination of wind and current can make trial-and-error the only method that guarantees access to a good fishing hole.

Once the anchor is let down to the bottom, it drags a certain distance before catching. While trying to stay over a ledge only a few yards in length—with the surface current going one way, the wind blowing another and the lines also being influenced by undersea currents—it's easy to lose sight of the fishing spot on the sonar screen. It's a great idea to motor above a reef several times and toss out floating marker buoys with weighted lines to mark the location of a ledge. By observing the row of markers, it's easier to anchor in a way to orient the boat directly above the ledge. By merely letting out or retrieving anchor line, the boat can be repositioned in reference to the markers until productive spots in the ledge are found and several areas of the ledge can be fished without having to raise the anchor or start the motor.

Chapter 10

Shrimp Boat Sharks

The salt air held so much water vapor that the mist-clouds squatting on the sea seemed as solid as the translucent doorway to a Swedish sauna. Even the artificial breeze generated by riding an open boat failed to evaporate layers of sweat and 100 percent humidity. Our shirts stuck to our backs while the boat rolled over the final whale's hump of a wave marking the outer limits of Carolina Beach Inlet.

The summer doldrums had set in solidly. The Atlantic was slick as a pool of melted candle wax. Not one ripple graced her surface to indicate the tiniest whisper of wind that would provide relief from the July heat. Unlike most summer fishing days that begin with a boat ride in the dark foredawn, this ride began well after sunrise, even though the air was so thick that the sun couldn't be identified except as a brighter zone of light glowing like a neon tube in the eastern region of the sky a few degrees above the horizon.

"Nothing's biting, so let's go shark fishing," had come the word on my cell phone the day before.

The call was from Captain Fisher Culbreth, who operates *Capture Charters* out of Carolina Beach. Indeed, the high water temperature had made most fish lethargic and, while there were still a few of nearly everything being caught, the easy fishing and massive catches typical of May and June had slowed to a trickle. I happened to be fruitlessly fishing for finicky flounder when the phone rang, so I jumped at the chance to hook up with Culbreth the next day.

The tide was falling as we left the inlet for open water. The shrimp boats were already hard at work, towing their nets to catch shrimp that gathered in high concentrations outside the inlet as the diminishing water level flushed them out of nearby marshes and channels.

Sea gulls and pelicans swarmed and dove around one of the boats in flocks so thick they looked like honeybees defending a hive from a marauding bear. The shrimp boat looked like an old lady lifting her skirts as she stepped over a mud puddle, with her nets hoisted high on either side and her steel-bound wooden doors flared wide.

"He's finishing a tow and dumping his catch," said Culbreth. "As soon as he starts culling, the sharks will come up right behind his boat."

The dorsal fins of porpoises rolled in the prop wash of the shrimper as Culbreth fell in behind. A pair of the sea mammals surfaced right in front of the bow as Culbreth brought the boat off plane to trolling speed. Spouting, the porpoises added their breath to the steam bath above the ocean's surface.

"Some people think that porpoises will attack sharks and keep them away," said Shawn Ashcroft as he removed a rod from the rocket launcher in the boat's T-top and set it into a rod holder in the port side of the stern. "But all the sharks and porpoises gather behind the shrimpers to eat when the catch is culled. The porpoises stay on top and the sharks stay deeper, so we just drop the baits down a little bit when porpoises are in the area."

Ashcroft serves as Culbreth's mate when he's needed and as his best friend all of the time. Since a tag team of three ups the odds when wrestling a huge shark from the ocean, he had come along to share in the competition. While he set out the baits and I wiped the steadily replenished supply of condensation from my sunglasses and camera lens, Culbreth fell in right behind the shrimp boat.

"Look! There's a blacktip!" shouted Culbreth.

We sighted along his pointing finger to a slashing boil within 5 feet of the stern of the shrimp boat. A gray dorsal fin with a black

Captain Fisher Culbreth of *Capture Charters* in Carolina Beach catches sharks by trolling behind shrimp boats as they cull their catch.

tip flashed above the surface, followed by a black-tipped tail that sprayed water all the way up to the deck of the shrimper, wetting the crew.

Other gulping splashes appeared here and there as we entered the riot of screeching gulls, breeching porpoises and slashing sharks. The thrum of the shrimp boat's engine and the animal noises added to the feeling of foreboding as we approached at a distance that seemed way too close to me.

"Look at the screen," Culbreth commanded, drawing my attention to his color scope that was mounted on top of the center console. "That structure you see on the bottom is the net."

Sure enough, as we had gained water on the shrimper, she had lowered her net and now we were right above it. The prop wash added a roll to the ocean and I asked Culbreth just how close was too close.

"When you feel the prop wash pulling you in toward the shrimp boat, you had better back off," he said. "I know all of these guys and they really don't mind someone who knows what they're doing fishing this close. They just want you to keep your lines out of the nets. If you get a hook hung in a net, you have to call the captain of the shrimp boat on the radio so the crew can watch out when the net is hauled in at the end of a tow. They have to haul the net in every hour to prevent any captured turtles from being drowned. When the net is dropped back into the water, the catch is culled and the discarded fish and squid bring the scavengers in to feed."

Ashcroft had rigged some baits while Culbreth idled the boat in trolling position. He dipped a whole 7-inch mullet into a pool of fish blood on top of an ice chest and impaled it through the head with a 9/0 hook. Crimped onto the hook was a 5-foot leader of 80-pound, seven-strand steel cable. A 6-ounce egg sinker was threaded onto the line above the leader's swivel to take the bait down to the fish.

"King mackerel tackle wears the sharks out too much," Culbreth said. "If they quit swimming, sharks will die. So we use tackle on the heavy side to catch sharks. I like to use a heavy boat rod and a 4/0 *Penn* reel spooled with 80-pound test line for sharks. The drag is set at about 15 pounds. It's a little hard on the fisherman, but it's easier on the sharks if you're going to release them."

Ashcroft set out the rod rigged with the whole mullet bait off one corner of the stern and its twin off the opposite corner. Into a rod holder at the center of the stern, he set a rod baited with a mullet fillet. While none of the baits were set far from the stern, the longest line was set first, the intermediate line set second and the shortest line set last to keep them from tangling.

"That mullet was so big, he made two good baits," Ashcroft said as the sinker made a splash behind the outboard motor. The fillet was about 9 inches long and Ashcroft had inserted the hook near the tip at the head end. He said that it would keep the fillet from spinning in the water and twisting the line or balling up the bait.

As the last bait was set out, Culbreth trolled right above the shrimp net. The first strike came within minutes.

The fish was a sandbar shark weighing about 50 pounds. When he struck, the rod bent like an archer's bow while the reel's clicker grudgingly ratcheted out line. Ashcroft pulled the rod from the holder with some difficulty because the pressure of the fish wedged the rod butt in place.

Culbreth eased his boat away from the shrimp boat while her crew hesitated in their culling duties to watch the fight. After the shark was far enough from the net to prevent a tangle, he strapped a fight belt around Ashcroft's waist. Ashcroft then increased the reel's drag tension to put greater pressure on the fish. Five minutes later, the shark's dorsal fin sliced the water near the boat.

Culbreth grabbed the leader and held the fish's head against the outer gunwale. Sliding a J-shaped, de-hooking tool that looked like a hay baling hook down the leader, he snagged the curve of the hook shank, gave it a twist and the fish swam away unharmed.

While sandbar sharks are the most common species in the area in mid-summer, there are other species caught behind the shrimp boats as well. The dusky shark is similar to a sandbar and the two species can be difficult to tell apart. The dusky has a dorsal fin set farther back, while the sandbar has a dorsal fin almost above the pectoral fins. Sandbar sharks average 50-100 pounds while dusky sharks average 250 pounds and can attain lengths of 8-10 feet. Blacktip sharks are similar in size to sandbar sharks and have distinctive black tips on their fins. These three species of sharks are likely to be caught behind shrimp boats, but there are larger and smaller prizes to be hooked as well.

Tiger sharks with their distinctive lateral stripes, and hammerhead sharks with their strange head shapes, are truly monsters of the deep and can weigh hundreds of pounds. In contrast, spiny dogfish and Atlantic sharpnose sharks usually weigh less than 15 pounds. Anglers can encounter all of these species by trolling behind a shrimp boat near Carolina Beach. Spiny dogfish have poisonous spines on their fin tips. They also make for fine eating, so anglers should learn to identify them by

Big sharks are strong fighters and have sharp teeth, making wire leaders the key to landing them.

looking for the spines.

After the first shark had been boated, Culbreth quickly motored back into the shrimper's wake. After several other sandbar sharks of up to 70 pounds in weight were fought and released, a huge fish bit right through a leader. For an instant its black-tipped dorsal fin sliced the surface, then the line went slack. The second reel sang and went silent, followed quickly by the third as the big fish fed. Culbreth grumbled to himself as he clipped the remnants of three 80-pound test, seven-strand leaders and tied on 200-pound, single-strand leaders in their places.

"It's difficult to imagine a fish that can cut 80-pound wire, but a big shark can do it easily," Culbreth said. "If a shark gets a bite on you, he won't let go and you'll lose whatever part of you he has a hold on."

The words would prove eerily prophetic on the next fish that struck. This time the baits were different. We had caught so many sharks that our bait supply was exhausted so Culbreth radioed the captain of the shrimp boat. The captain was kind enough to float some of the culled finfish over the side in a plastic bag.

Retrieved with a gaff, the cull included mostly squid, spots, croakers and pinfish. There was also a scattering of undersized weakfish and speckled trout that Culbreth quickly tossed overboard. Having undersized fish—even as dead cull for bait—aboard a sport fishing boat is illegal.

The next fish to strike was a sandbar shark of about 50 pounds in weight. I asked Culbreth to hold the shark still for a photo. While he held the leader perpendicular to the water and used the de-hooking tool to steady the wire, the apparently exhausted fish found renewed energy and leapt into the boat.

Thankfully, the leader held. Culbreth used the de-hooker to deflect the shark and the clenching jaws clamped down on air an inch or two from his leg. He led the shark back over the side with the leader and twisted the hook free. Letting out an uneasy chuckle, he resumed his place at the wheel.

"Trying to save a shark can get risky and is not for amateurs," Culbreth said. "That was a close call. On a really big shark, it's a good idea to snip the leader as near the hook as possible. By using a hook and leader that will rust when shark fishing, anglers can play it safe and save the shark, along with their own body parts."

Sharks are good to eat, with the dogfish and sandbar sharks especially nice in flavor and texture. Anglers who want to boat sharks should play the fish to unconsciousness and further subdue the fish with a blow to the head before securing it in a sturdy ice chest or fish box. However, recreational shark fishing regulations are very complex and anglers should learn to identify shark species and check with the NCDMF for current regulations.

Additional Information

Captain Fisher Culbreth operates *Capture Charters* out of Carolina Beach. Anglers can contact him at (910) 262-1450.

John Gillilan and Phil Pare won the battle with this big
amberjack.

Chapter 11

Jacked Around by A.J.'s

While having a door-slammed king mackerel live bait rod inspected by one of old Carolina Beach's most dedicated rod builders, I struck up a conversation with him about the many ways in which fine rods are broken. We rested in the shade of a tree and shared a can of soda. In spite of the shade, the July heat vaporized the droplets of condensation the instant they dropped from the can and hit the pavement of his driveway.

"Rods are seldom broken by fish. It's generally the fisherman who does the damage to his equipment," Terry Dingler said. "But if a real brute of a fish like an amberjack takes the rod tip down to the point where an the angler is on his knees and he just rests the rod on the side of the boat for an instant, the excess pressure can make it snap at the point of contact with the gunwale."

Since I was a fresh arrival to the saltwater from inland lakes and rivers that day 25 years ago, the thought of catching such a monster of a fish intrigued my imagination. So I asked Dingler for the scoop on catching what he liked to call an "A.J."

"When it's hot like this, the king mackerel aren't doing much near shore," Dingler said. "But there are schools of A.J.'s on the artificial reef off Kure Beach that beat anything I've ever seen. They're huge and easy to hook. Winning the battle is another thing entirely."

The next Saturday's sunrise caught my boss and fishing buddy, Joey Hill, and I motoring out of Carolina Beach Inlet in his 19-foot Grady White boat. Less than 3 miles south, we found the buoy that marked AR-378 by taking a compass course of 184 degrees off the inlet's sea buoy.

We had caught a livewell full of menhaden and mullets by casting a net in the Carolina Beach Boat Basin. I used a knife to cut some of them into chunks as Dingler had instructed. Dropping them into a bucket and adding a liberal dose of menhaden oil, I stirred them with the knife blade until the chunks were well greased, then began dropping them in a trail over the transom.

Hill navigated around the buoy in a circle while I rigged a live bait on a king mackerel rig. Instead of the standard two No. 4 treble hooks, this rig was tied with a pair of heavier No. 2 treble hooks. Thanks to a tip from Dingler, the 68-pound single-strand wire leader was twice the weight I normally used for catching king mackerel.

Not another boat was in sight. Such is the case when anglers learn a popular fishing hole has been taken over by amberjacks. They ruin live bait rigs, take hours to bring in and are not relished for eating along the North Carolina coast like they are in other parts of the South.

As we began our second circuit around the buoy, an A.J. hammered a chunk of menhaden floating on the surface. Hill ducked the geyser of water the A.J. splashed into the cockpit of the boat.

"Chumming up A.J.'s is as easy as feeding goldfish," Dingler had said.

His assessment was accurate. Violent thrashing at the surface gave the giant fish away. Looking down into the emerald water, we could see dozens of fish that had been lured upward from the submerged reef circling the bait cascading down through the water column.

I hooked a live menhaden and splashed it over the side. As I engaged the reel, a massive golden-brown fish engulfed the bait not 3 feet from the side of the boat. It was the most vicious topwater strike I had ever seen.

"Ease the boat away from the buoy," I asked of the captain. While we idled along, the fish just seemed to stay in one place while the drag rationed out 20-pound test monofilament line.

After we had moved 100 yards or so, the fish began to panic.

We had pulled him away from his comfort zone surrounding the reef. When he realized something was wrong, he surged back toward the structure. I increased the drag to about half the weight of the line. But when the fish ran, it seemed like we had hooked a submarine. Stopping his run was out of the question.

Patiently, as Dingler had instructed, we played the fish. Sometimes, he took the line almost back to the buoy. Sometimes, he slugged it out right under the boat. Eventually we drifted the fish away from the structure to open water. An hour into the battle, the captain yawned and cut off the motor. After the first dozen times, he had grown bored of hearing me say, "I think he's giving up now." Each time the fish neared the boat and sensed its presence in the water, he took another 50 yards of line, returned to the bottom and continued the fight.

Uninitiated in battling A.J.s, we hadn't heeded Dingler's advice for everyone besides the angler onboard to "pack along a big lunch and bring a book to read."

Ignoring another tip from Dingler, I increased the drag tension. The bend in the rod became too extreme; the rod touched the gunwale for a couple of seconds and snapped just above the first guide, above the point of Dingler's expert repair job. Fortunately, at this point the fish was nearly whipped, because I still managed to land it.

When I took the two pieces of the rod back to Dingler later, he said I was the first angler he'd ever heard of who'd landed a citation-sized A.J. with only half a rod. When the fish came alongside, I felt more relief than elation at catching the 50-plus-pound fish. I freed the hook with pliers and sent the tired sentinel back to guard his reef.

Next, it was Hill's turn. After a 2 1/2-hour battle he boated a fish we estimated to weigh far in excess of 70 pounds. Those two fish were enough. Muscle sore, hot and tired, we called it a day and headed home.

It has become a ritual in the years since. I always catch at least one amberjack when they show up, just to remember what it's like

Captain Bruce Trujillo of *Tight Loop Charters* at Wrightsville Beach caught this amberjack by using fly tackle at an artificial reef.

to hook up with a brown submarine, hang on and wait for it to give up or break the line.

There are many other places that amberjack may show up in

numbers along the Southeast coast. However, over the last 15 years or so, their numbers have been in decline. For king mackerel anglers, it seems to be a good thing because they don't waste time fighting huge brutes that make a shambles of carefully tied rigs. Most king fishermen tighten down their drags to break off the hooks if they think they've hooked an A.J.

I've seen amberjacks arrive in numbers at the north jetty of Masonboro Inlet, at AR-370, and at AR-382. They can show up as early as May, but the height of summer seems to be the best time to catch them. Folks living at the beach can become heroes to their guests visiting from inland. By hooking them up to an amberjack, they guarantee bragging rights back at home for their guests who have caught a true monster of the deep.

One way I've found to make the event even more of a thrill is chumming up a school until the fish are surface feeding. The sight of a dozen huge amberjacks hitting bait on top is such an incredible spectacle it's worth the effort just to feed them, even if you don't want to catch them. It can also be so unnerving when the water splashes right into the boat as an A.J. hits nearby that an inexperienced angler may back out of hooking up with such a strong fish. However, for the undaunted angler who wants to test his endurance and tackle to their limits, a large, white bucktail jig cast on spinning gear into the boiling water will easily attract a strike.

Captain Bruce Trujillo of *Tight Loop Charters* is even bold enough to test his fly tackle against an A.J. He makes a commotion with large poppers to attract the huge fish, and strikes usually come as the fly is stripped to within a few feet of the rod tip.

Mike Coleman, a Carolina Beach angler who's hooked many amberjacks over the years and once owned *Zora's Seafood* in downtown Wilmington, said, "As soon as people in Atlanta and other large cities across the South began to eat amberjack, the huge schools of big fish began to disappear. Around here, people don't eat amberjack because they have small, white parasitic worms in their meat in such numbers that they can't be cut out. I never sold amberjack in the fish market. But in states south of here, they're smoked to disguise the parasites, which won't do any harm to humans when cooked and eaten."

Coleman caught one of the first amberjacks I ever saw when he took me king mackerel fishing at AR-370 on his 20-foot Aquasport boat, *Mad Dog*. It was a monster of a fish that took 1 1/2 hours to boat on 20-pound class king mackerel gear. On the same trip, he caught a small A.J. of about 18 inches in length. Today any amberjack must be 28 inches, fork length, to be retained by a recreational angler in North Carolina. The bag limit is one fish per angler, per day. The restrictive regulations may eventually bring the big schools back to the Carolina coast, but back in the 1970s any numbers and any sizes of amberjacks could be kept.

Since the fish was small, we took it back to the dock for eating. Coleman believed the young fish wouldn't contain as many parasites as the large fish that are normally caught from the waters near Wrightsville Beach. We cleaned the fish and cut around the worms. There was a great deal of waste, with over half the meat lost because of our surgery, but the remaining flesh was very white and delicious after being cut into chunks and fried. We also fired up the charcoal in a smoker grill and found smoked A.J. to be worth the effort of catching the fish.

With today's angler limited to larger fish that usually have lots of parasites, North Carolina anglers release nearly all the fish they catch. I think it's a good thing. Although I still haven't seen the big schools of decades ago, there are still enough A.J.'s around to make me head out each season and get "jacked around" by at least one of the big brutes to prove that landing one on light tackle can still be done. To find them, I visit tackle shops and listen on the VHF radio for tales of amberjacks guarding a wreck or reef and keeping the king mackerel anglers away.

Additional Information

Captain Bruce Trujillo operates *Tight Loop Charters* out of Wrightsville Beach and specializes in catching nearshore game fish with fly tackle and light tackle.

He can be contacted at (910) 392-2786.

Phil Pare churned this big Spanish mackerel up from the depths by twitching a shiny surface lure.

Chapter 12

Churning Up Deep-Running Spanish Mackerel

Spanish mackerel are one of North Carolina's top game fish because they're good to eat and easy to catch. Well, usually they're easy to catch. There are times when these speedy fish can be maddening devils nearly impossible to fool into striking a hook.

The trolling routine used by most offshore anglers can put lots of fish in the boat when they're cooperative and form large schools that can easily be spotted at the surface. When birds swoop down from the sky to feed upon baitfish that are chased to the top by masses of hungry Spanish mackerel, anglers trolling spoons have just as easy pickings as the aerial predators.

However, as light penetration increases with the angle of the sun, Spanish mackerel head deep. On hot days, high water temperature can also keep them near the bottom, even at dawn and dusk when they're usually most active at the surface. On other days, the fish just don't want to cooperate by striking spoons trolled on top—although they jump all around the boat and frustrate anglers by giving only an occasional strike or none at all. Anglers who can't get the idea of trolling with spoons to catch Spanish mackerel out of their minds generally bring out the heavy trolling rods and use planers to get their spoons down into the strike zone. When the fish are deep you have to troll where the fish are in the water column. When they're merely being persnickety, fishing deeper works better because lure-shy fish don't have enough light to make out imposters and leaders and are more easily duped into striking.

Trolling spoons behind planers can certainly be effective at such times. But for the dedicated light tackle sport fishermen, the hassle of setting out large planers on heavy tackle to catch small fish turns into a chore of meat fishing. When using rods and reels suitable for planers, anglers don't get to fight the fish. The planers necessary to take lures down to the bottom are often so heavy that the angler is merely reeling in the planer with the fish attached to it by the leader and spoon. Instead of resorting to heavy gear, anglers who use the right lures and techniques can still jig Spanish mackerel to the top when they head down deep.

Jeff Stokley has lived in Wilmington from the day he was born. I was with Stokley fishing near the old site of Corncake Inlet below Fort Fisher on a hot day in May.

Stokley targets the hard bottom area beginning just northeast of the old inlet site. The inlet has now shifted south several miles and is closed off by sand erosion, but Sheephead Rock still appears on navigation charts and is the place to start looking for Spanish mackerel.

"The rock formation only begins near Sheephead Rock," Stokley said. "It continues in a northeasterly direction for several miles, right on up to Kure Beach. The water is really shallow right on top of Sheephead Rock. When the water is clear and the sun is bright, you can actually look down into the water and see the rock formation 12 feet below. As it continues northeastward, the formation becomes deeper at up to 30 feet. On either side the water drops off to over 40 feet in places. Spanish mackerel are usually located right on top of the ledges or just off to either side."

Stokley first ran into schools of big Spanish mackerel while jigging with heavy jigging spoons for gray trout. Though most gray trout bites taper off as the water temperature rises with the coming of spring, there are always a few that stay late.

"When looking for grays, I use a depthfinder to spot the fish," said Stokley. "They're always right on the bottom. But while I was watching the screen, there were a few birds diving. Occasional small schools of Spanish and individual fish were cutting bait at the surface. I didn't pay them much attention since I was looking for gray trout. I spotted a school of fish on the screen and shut off the motor."

Stokley allowed the boat to drift through the area while he kept an eye on the screen. Dropping a silver *Gibbs Minnow* jigging spoon to the bottom, he twitched it up and down.

The fish hit the spoon savagely and took off at a streaking run. Stokley knew right away that the fish was not a gray trout.

"I thought I had a bluefish," Stokley said. "But after a couple of fast, long runs, I pumped a huge Spanish mackerel to the boat."

Stokley then tried trolling the area with *Clarkspoons*. However, the fish were scattered and he drew scant strikes from small fish. It didn't take long for him to return to the same area where he had located the deep school of fish on the depthfinder.

"Everyone, my son Shawn and cousin Bobby Huckabee, rigged up with jigging spoons. We used *Hopkins*, *Stingsilvers* and *Gibbs* spoons. They all seemed to work well."

The beauty of using a jigging spoon for catching Spanish according to Stokley, is that they reach the bottom quickly. They also cheat the wind and are easy to cast long distances.

"When the wind's blowing, I like to anchor the boat on top of a school," Stokley said. "When the boat's drifting, I don't get to fish as much because I have to constantly re-start the motor and navigate back to the fish. While everyone else catches fish, it cuts down on my fishing time. Spanish aren't bottom fish like gray trout. They move around a lot. They may not remain right on the bottom. You can watch them move up and down on the depthfinder and see the fish surface. With a heavy jigging spoon, you can present it at the right depth and you can also cast to visible fish. If the fish move away from the boat, you can usually relocate them by casting all around the boat."

By casting around the boat methodically when the bite tapers off, anglers can quickly find the fish that have moved away but are still oriented around the structure. The clock-face method used by largemouth bass anglers is the quickest way to find the fish. By beginning at the stern at 6 o'clock and working clockwise all around the boat, a crew quickly finds the fish that have moved away by using 1 1/2 to 2-ounce jigging spoons that be can cast 50 yards.

Phil Pare is another veteran of Wilmington's saltwater fishing. He specializes in catching fish on light spinning tackle.

"I hate trolling," Pare said. "I like to feel the fish when it strikes and I like to play the fish all the way to the boat. Trolling takes the fun out of catching Spanish mackerel."

Pare tries to spot fish on top when he heads out Masonboro Inlet, but he doesn't despair if he doesn't see fish or if the inlet is covered with boats trolling heavy planer rods. He works the area near the jetties with a white bucktail jig. He usually uses a small jig weighing 1/4 of an ounce.

"One mistake most fishermen make with Spanish is using lures that are too big," Pare said. "When the fish are picky about what lures they hit, it means they're feeding on small baitfish."

Pare casts the jig and lets it sink. Sometimes the fish hit the lure on the way down, but they usually want it moving at a good clip.

"You can't reel a lure fast enough to take it away from a Spanish mackerel," Pare said. "A Spanish is a fast-moving fish and he likes to eat on the run."

Another lure Pare uses is a called a tinsel jig, a lead-head jig body with a Mylar skirt. The jig has a lot more flash from reflected sunlight than a jig dressed with hair.

"I like to use red-and-white, and blue-and-white tinsel jigs," Pare said. "But it pays to have several colors along because the fish can also be picky about color."

As the day heats up and action declines near the inlet, Pare heads to the deep hole between Masonboro Inlet and the Oceanic Pier. Spanish mackerel congregate in the hole as light penetration and the surface water temperatures increase.

"If the fish are there, there'll be charter boats in the area trolling planers and catching fish," Pare said. "I try to stay out of their trolling pattern and circle the area until I find a school on the depthfinder or with the jigs."

I was along with Pare when he shared another secret lure for catching Spanish when they're deep. We had been jigging up a few fish in the deep hole. The wind was up and we drifted along while casting. At first, Pare was casting a red-and-white tinsel jig and I was using a gold *Gibbs* spoon.

Above all else Pare likes action when he fishes. He constantly tries something new if the fishing is slow. But of all things to try out for catching fish that were holding in 25 feet of water, Pare tied on a surface lure!

Pare cast a floating *Yo-Zuri* minnow that was red-and-white, the same colors as the tinsel jig he had been using. Since the boat was drifting along in front of the wind, the lightweight lure didn't go very far. But he kept the bail open on the spinning reel and allowed the line to extend about 20 yards behind the boat.

Instead of retrieving the lure with a steady beat, he began to twitch it hard while slowly turning on the reel handle. After each twitch, he let the lure rest.

The water was very clear and I saw fish as they streaked toward the surface from below to attack the lure. The first Spanish struck with absolute fury. Never have I witnessed such a viscous strike from a Spanish mackerel.

While I fruitlessly continued to probe the depths with the spoon, Pare continued to have action. He made fewer casts but was catching more fish, so I decided to give it a try.

"The key is the flash," Pare said. "There's something about the *Yo-Zuri* that makes it reflect sunlight down into the water. When you twitch the lure it rolls over on its side and acts like a mirror. The fish see the flash and come to the surface to hit it. It works best with full sunlight."

Pare gave me a *Yo-Zuri* lure and I began casting and twitching it on the surface. It turned out that he had been doing less casting than me but doing more work. The speed it took to turn on the fish from so deep took effort, but the lures were light enough that I could keep up the pace. I found that this method is easier if the angler keeps the line straight out in front and lifts the rod tip straight up, or if he keeps his body perpendicular to the line coming off the rod tip from right to left and twitches the rod along the same plane as the water (for a right-handed angler). Reeling with the line coming off the rod tip from left to right made it difficult to keep the lure moving fast enough.

Eventually, the size of the fish and the ferocity of their strikes took its toll on the lightweight lures, which were being pressed beyond their intended purpose. The plastic lip on the front of Pare's *Yo-Zuri* minnow was shattered by the strike of a big Spanish and the mono leader I was using was clipped by their razor-sharp teeth.

With the two most productive lures out of commission, we headed back to the inlet with forearms knotted from jigging spoons and twitching lures, but mostly from fighting big Spanish mackerel called up from their deep-water sanctuary. As we passed some trolling anglers playing tug-o-war with their heavy gear, Phil remarked that they were probably more tired than we were since they were reeling in No. 4 planers on heavy trolling rods to catch the same-sized fish.

"There's no way they're having more fun than we did today," Pare said.

I just grinned and wrote a mental tackle shop list for replenishing his stock of flashy lures.

Chapter 13

State Record Spadefish

Charles Dycus lives to fish. He likes coastal fishing so much that he closes down his taxidermy shop, *Plank Road Taxidermy*, in Sanford for several weeks during the summer to fish the Southport area for a wide variety of saltwater species.

Dycus personally caught the state record black drum, weighing 101.1 pounds, in 1998, but seldom does he fish alone. Instead he brings family and friends from back home to share his fishing adventures.

Two of his fellow anglers caught state record fish of a different species during August within two days of one another. On August 4, 2001, his daughter, Emily, caught a spadefish weighing 8.22 pounds.

"Spadefish fight hard," Dycus said. "It really put up a good tussle. Once we got back to the dock, we weighed the fish in. We called the North Carolina Division of Marine Fisheries to find out what the state record was. It took them a while to look it up, but the old state record was 8 pounds, 2 ounces. Emily's fish weighed 8.22 pounds, which was a couple of ounces more."

But Emily Dycus' state record would stand for only a couple of days. On August 6, 2001, Charles Dycus had Spencer Smith, Tommy Brewer and his wife, Janice Brewer onboard. Tommy Brewer had hooked a huge spadefish and was fighting it when Smith hooked another one.

"I had to put my pole under the anchor rope to keep the line from cutting off," Smith said. "Then my line got wrapped up in Tommy's line and his fish got cut off."

Smith fought the fish for 4 or 5 minutes. When it came to the

Emily Dycus' potential state record spadefish was short-lived. (Photo by Charles Dycus).

boat, it was the biggest spadefish anyone onboard had ever seen. When it was weighed on the scales at *Wildlife Bait and Tackle* in Southport, its weight was certified at 9.05 pounds, surpassing the state record set two days before on the same boat.

"I fish three or four times each summer with Charles," Smith said. "We were fishing for black drum in the Cape Fear River, but the black drum weren't biting, so we headed out to the reefs to catch a few spadefish. We like to eat the spadefish. The meat is about like that of a sheepshead. It cooks up white and tastes very good."

Dycus had taken his friends and family to the Yaupon Beach Artificial Reef, AR-425. He said there are also fish on the McGlammery Artificial Reef, AR-420.

Spencer Smith caught the state record spadefish by using a jelly ball for bait.

"We had been catching lots of fish in the 5- to 7-pound weight range," Dycus said. But we had no idea of what the state record was. There are probably even bigger fish on the Brunswick reefs."

Spadefish resemble super-sized aquarium angelfish. Their profile is shaped like a garden shovel and they have wide

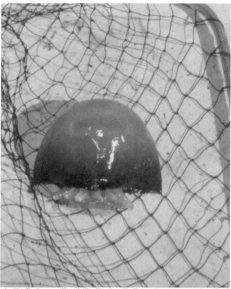

Jellyfish, called "jelly balls" or "cannon balls," make the best bait for catching spadefish.

alternating black and silver bands on their sides running from the top to the bottom. Dycus and his companions catch the big spadefish by using a teaser made of a stringer of a round, harmless jellyfish called locally "cannonballs" or "jelly balls." These pinkish or purplish jellyfish are common in the area during the hot months of summer and form huge schools. They can easily be dipped from the ocean with a landing net.

"We string a teaser, which is a daisy chain of about five or six jelly balls onto a fish stringer," Dycus said. "Then we tie on a 12-ounce sinker below them and let it down to about 15 feet for a while. Spadefish feed on jellyfish and they'll follow the daisy chain up to the surface when it's raised back up. Sometimes we also chum with shrimp, jellyfish and clams to keep the fish on top and draw them close to the boat."

To catch the fish, Dycus uses cut jellyfish mantles or whole jellyfish for bait. He ties a three-way swivel to the line and ties two No. 2 snelled *Eagle Claw* bait-holder hooks to the swivel. A 1/2-ounce bank sinker below the hooks takes the bait down to the fish and helps in casting. One of the hooks on Smith's state record fish was imbedded in the fish's mouth and the other in its tail. Both hooks had been imbedded into a whole jelly ball that was used as bait.

Dycus uses a medium action, 6-foot spinning rod with a *Penn 1500* spinning reel spooled with 10-pound test monofilament line to catch spadefish. The fish put up a good fight on the light tackle.

"They can run from 8 feet to 35 feet quicker than the blink of your eye," Smith said. "A lot of spadefish get cut off on the structure of the reef when they go deep. You just have to keep the pressure on the fish and hope the line doesn't snag the reef."

David Franklin with a big dolphin caught along a weed line offshore of Morehead City.

Chapter 14

Dolphin Dash Chases the Doldrums Away

The peak of summer can be a finicky time for fish and a frustrating time for offshore anglers. High surface water temperatures make many fish lethargic or force them to head for cooler climes. High air temperatures make anglers sluggish or choose to stay in port. Adding an easterly wind to the summer doldrums that can set in during July and August keeps anglers "on the hill" for days at a time.

There's an old saying along the Carolina coast that goes, "When the wind's from the east, the fish bite the least." There's much truth to the old adage. But with one popular game fish, it's not necessarily so.

An easterly wind that blows for several days moves creeping masses of sargassum seaweed inshore of its usual home in the Gulf Stream and with it, one of Neptune's most perfect sea creatures. Dolphin are legendary for their incredible speed, aerial acrobatics and are arguably the most beautiful fish that anglers can catch fishing from mackerel boats. They also offer culinary fare that's fit for gourmets and are extremely prolific and fast growing. It's no wonder dolphin are highly prized by anglers. By paying attention to the wind and scouting the positions of weed lines, anglers can break the spell of the fishing doldrums by making a dolphin dash when it moves near shore.

Dolphin sometimes move to within 5 miles of the beach, but are more typically caught in mackerel boats at a range of 20 to 30 miles out. The fish are ravenous feeders and reach adult weights exceeding 40 pounds at less than 1 year of age. Mature male "bulls" have characteristic high vertical foreheads, while the smaller female "cows" have rounded foreheads.

While dolphin can exceed 100 pounds in weight, it's rare to catch a large dolphin inside the Gulf Stream, which is typically oriented more than 50 miles west of the Carolina coast in summer. Juvenile dolphin of up to 20 pounds are the primary catch of king mackerel boat anglers and they can be caught by using several techniques.

Besides finding masses of floating weed, the presence of flying fish indicates the presence of dolphin. Anytime a boat is traveling near a weed line and flying fish leap from the water, startled by the boat, the anglers onboard should check the area for dolphin. Flying fish are the top forage fish for dolphin, and anglers who ply Gulf Stream waters troll lures that imitate flying fish when targeting dolphin.

Trolling at 5 to 7 knots along the edge of a weed line while pulling trolling skirts and rigged ballyhoos can be a productive tactic anywhere dolphin are feeding. However, this method burns a lot of fuel, and fuel can be a carefully rationed commodity for a king mackerel boat—especially if the fish are located offshore at the extreme limits of fuel consumption range. Slowing down and adapting tactics specific to the habits of dolphin is a great way for getting in on the action from smaller craft.

Dolphin will strike king mackerel baits that are slow-trolled on king mackerel live bait rigs. Slow-trolling live menhaden and frozen ballyhoo or cigar minnows entices dolphin to the hook nearly as well as fast-trolling techniques with high-speed lures.

Once a dolphin is hooked, it's a good idea to leave at least one other line in the water. Dolphin are schooling fish and will often bring other fish along as they're played to the boat. As the hooked fish nears the boat any baits remaining in the water could be struck by tag-along fish.

Smaller fish typically caught by anglers inshore of the Gulf Stream are often called "shingles" or "bailers." The term "shingle" indicates the size of the fish as about that of a house roof shingle, while "bailer" identifies a telltale habit of the juvenile schooling fish that can lead to some fast action on light tackle.

When the water is clear, an angler can look into its depths and see schooling dolphin as they near the boat following a hooked fish. There are other situations and places where anglers can spot schools of dolphin. Any type of floating debris or large, slow-moving sea life such as whale sharks and sea turtles can attract dolphin. A boat at anchor during a bottom fishing expedition is one of the best dolphin attractors in the ocean if a weed line is present; the water is hot and the fish are in the area.

When schooling fish are spotted down in the water or seen while they chase baitfish at the surface, hooking a fish and playing it to the boat is the first priority. The first fish is then tied off near the transom where it performs like a decoy to attract other fish in the school. Light spinning tackle can be used to catch these schooling juvenile fish. Often the action is so fast that the small fish are hooked, reeled in and hauled into the boat by swinging them aboard, giving rise to the term "bailing" dolphin.

Jigs can be cast and allowed to sink to the level of fish that are spotted in deep water. Once the fish are attracted to the jig or spoon, they're retrieved as rapidly as the reel handle will turn. No lure can swim faster than a dolphin, so the lure can't be retrieved too quickly.

If fish follow the lure but don't strike, they're at least brought nearer the surface, and dolphin are surface-feeding experts. Since their staple prey is flying fish, using a lure or bait to imitate a flying fish is sure to result in a hook-up.

A small, flashy spoon or sparkling tinsel jig cast at a low angle so it skips a time or two before it dips below the surface will attract the attention of dolphin. Popping plugs that disrupt the surface then sink when allowed to rest are also great lures for bailing dolphin. After leaping from the water and re-entering, it takes a moment for a flying fish to regenerate enough momentum to make another leap. It's at this moment that dolphin time their attack. By working their lures to imitate this flaw in the escape tactics of flying fish, anglers can stimulate and exploit the feeding response in dolphin.

When hooked on light spinning tackle, small dolphin leap just like the adult fish. The neon greens, yellows and blues of a dolphin as it clears the water are a sight that must be seen, first-hand, to be appreciated. No camera's film or lens can capture the luster of a lit-up dolphin, fresh from the sea.

Chapter 15

Beach Blanket Flounder on Nearshore Reefs

The coast of North Carolina may have the best fishing for big flounder of any place in the country. Although large numbers of nice-sized fish weighing from 2 to 4 pounds are caught beginning in late May, it's the period from late August through early September that the really big, citation-sized fish of over 5 pounds show up in strength.

The run of huge flounder is coast-wide in the state. However, several factors come into play that make the southeastern coast of North Carolina the very best place to try for a beach-towel-sized fish. Several flounder are caught from the area each season that run from 10 to 16 pounds in weight, and the state record flounder, weighing 20 pounds, 8 ounces was caught in the region. The Cape Fear River influences the area with its fertile discharge into the ocean, which fattens the mullet and menhaden that live in the river with phytoplankton. In turn, flounder feast on the baitfish.

Ocean bag limits were established to protect summer flounder during the 1990s, and they have also helped protect Southern flounder from over-harvest. They have also helped increase the numbers of big Southern flounder that are the mainstay of most Carolina coastal flat-fisherman. Flounder limits are subject to frequent changes and anglers should contact the North Carolina Division of Marine Fisheries in Morehead City for current limits.

Captain Wayne Freeman is one of the top guides around Southport. A day with Freeman, who operates *Flatfish Charters*, can result in over a dozen fine flounder for his clients.

Captain Wayne Freeman of *Flatfish Charters* in Southport catches lots of "doormat" flounder at artificial reefs.

The first time I met Freeman, he was introduced to me as "Rerun." He said the nickname was a holdover from his younger days when the way he listened to taped rock and roll music over and over was the subject of teasing from his buddies. But, after fishing with Freeman, I'm sure the nickname stuck with him into adulthood because of the way his clients repeatedly bring huge flatfish over the side of the boat.

Freeman fishes bucktail jigs around the face of the islands at the Cape Fear River mouth above Southport. He casts 5/8-ounce bucktail jigs with mullet minnows hooked on as teasers.

"The trick is casting to the little indentations along the grass beds," said Freeman while unhooking a fish caught on his first cast. "Flounder face the grass and wait in those pockets for baitfish to swim by."

It seems all the Southport guides have different techniques for fishing a bucktail. I tried to match the shimmy of his retrieve and found it difficult to maintain over a long period of time. It takes plenty of wrist action to force flounder into striking at the high rates of success that Freeman seeks.

"I work the bucktail along the bottom and keep it vibrating," said Freeman. "The more action you give it, the more strikes it will draw. The combination of wriggling the lure and the live mullet trailer drives fish wild. Any fish in the area will be caught when you cover all the water within casting distance in a methodical manner."

After fanning an area with casts and retrieves, Freeman pulls the anchor and drifts or motors to another likely spot to repeat the process. By covering lots of water, he systematically mines fish from area after area.

He also likes to fish deep oyster beds on the eastern side of the Cape Fear River. Offshore craft must use caution in the area and fish only on the higher tides to avoid touching bottom.

"Flounder like to lie on top of the oyster beds or near them," Freeman said. "But snagging oysters with bucktails can get expensive when the line cuts on the shells. I swim the jig and constantly vibrate and move it up and down across the top of the beds, trying to keep the lure 1 to 2 feet above the bottom. The fish come up off the bottom to strike the lure and I avoid hang-ups."

In selecting a bucktail jig, Freeman said to find one with a round head that has a durable paint job. He likes white jigs with painted eyes. For casting artificial lures, he uses 10-pound test

Vicky Rae Fredrick with a big flounder caught just offshore of Wrightsville Beach.

monofilament line.

Offshore, Freeman likes to fish the Yaupon Reef. The reef is located near the Cape Fear River mouth.

Using a depthfinder, Freeman studied the structure until he

found an uneven bottom perhaps 20 yards west of the AR-425 Buoy. As I slipped the anchor over the side and to the bottom, the line tightened as the boat swung its bow into the wind.

"I lost an anchor here yesterday," Freeman said. "One of the most important things to have aboard when fishing the reef is a spare anchor because they can get hung and lost on all the structure."

Freeman tied on a No. 6 style, 42 wide-bend *Eagle Claw* hook to the end of a 17-pound test monofilament leader. Above the hook, he tied on a 1 1/2-ounce bank sinker using a dropper loop. The leader was tied to the 10-pound test main line using a 60-pound swivel.

"I like the small hook because it draws more strikes," Freeman said. "If I'm using larger baits than finger mullet, I may go to a larger hook. The trick is to keep the hook small enough compared to the bait size to keep the fish from noticing the hook."

We hooked and landed fish weighing up to the citation size of 5 pounds. When the action tapered off, Freeman hoisted the anchor and moved a few feet to another location.

"You have to fish near the structure," Freeman said. "Flounder lie in the sand at the base of the structure and wait for the baitfish to swim out for an easy meal. If you fish right on the structure, you get hung up a lot and lose rigs."

It wasn't long before we had a limit of fish and had to head back to port. Where once flounder were considered a mainstay of inshore anglers, the return of the ocean populations of summer flounder has created a fantastic fishery for offshore boats.

The size and bag limits for ocean flounder have translated into doormats returning to the reefs. The addition of Reef Balls to many of the state's nearshore artificial reefs, including Yaupon Reef, has resulted in an increase in the number of big flounder. Anglers fishing for flounder in ocean waters near artificial reefs are advised to carry large diameter landing nets, with 24 inches in width a minimum size.

In addition to doormats, there are always a few beach blankets around. Who knows? The next state record flounder may just come from one of the nearshore artificial reefs.

Additional Information

Captain Wayne Freeman operates *Flatfish Charters* out of Southport. Anglers can contact him at (910) 457-5038.

Chapter 16

Tarpon by the Ton

Mark Miller has caught many types of fish in his recreational angling "career." Like most saltwater anglers, the Wilmington sportsman went through phases when he pursued king mackerel, striped bass, grouper and other well-known species. However, while fishing at the southern tip of Bald Head Island one night nearly 3 decades ago, Miller and his companions Ken Corbett and John Weaver hooked up with 46 tarpon—but landed only four of them. Many of the fish exceeded 100 pounds in weight. The fish they hooked, fought, landed and lost had an aggregate weight estimated at 2 tons!

"Instead of hooking those tarpon, the fish hooked me," Miller said. "Now, the only reason I keep up a boat is to jump some tarpon."

Miller's hook-up-to-catch ratio seems feeble to the uninformed angler, until some research reveals that a 10 to 1 proportion of strikes to landed fish is typical for such a hard-to-hook fish. A tarpon has a bony mouth that defies hook penetration. There are two theories on selecting hooks that hold securely enough to boat the fish. One is the use of a straight-shank hook and the other is the use of a circle hook.

"Some anglers use circle hooks, but I like a 6/0 to 8/0 straight-shank hook," said Miller. "I use 3 feet of 100-pound monofilament leader tied to the line with a 150-pound swivel. On the line above the swivel, I just use the metal clip taken off a fish-finder slide to attach a 3 or 4-ounce bank sinker to carry the bait to the bottom. The plastic slides are more expensive and you can lose several in a night's fishing. I'd rather lose nickels than dollars."

The night bite was right at Bald Head Island when Tom Gore caught this big tarpon.

Miller uses *Penn* reels in sizes from 940 to 6/0 matched with heavyweight rods spooled with 50-pound test monofilament. With this heavy tackle, he can land a tarpon of up to 100 pounds after a fight that lasts from 15 minutes to 1 hour.

He sets a light drag and leaves the warning clicker on when waiting for a strike. At the strike, he tightens the drag and hauls back on the rod to drive the hook into the mouth of the fish.

"Usually, he has the bait in his mouth when he jumps," Miller said. "There's slack in the line while he's in the air, so you don't know which rod he's on until he hits the water and the reel goes off. That's when it really gets exciting."

For bait, Miller uses whole or halved spots or chunks of bluefish. He has his best luck when he's catching lots of bluefish in the area where he's tarpon fishing and uses the bluefish for bait.

"I fish in the sloughs right off the tip of Bald Head Island between the sand lumps of the shoals," Miller said. "There's usually more action on the ocean side. But if it's rough in the ocean, I fish the Cape Fear River side of the shoals."

Miller said the roughest conditions usually occur during a northeasterly wind or during a thunderstorm. When he sees a storm coming up he usually has about 30 minutes to move his 20-foot Wellcraft boat to sheltered water. He said a southwest wind means poor tarpon fishing because it sends stained river water through the sloughs that prevents tarpon from seeing well enough to feed on baitfish.

The best conditions for catching tarpon occur during the August full moon when the water is calm. Miller sets up at sunset. Then he watches the moon rise over the ocean.

"There's not a prettier place to anchor up and wait," Miller said. "Listening to the birds that are sitting on the sand lumps and watching the moon shimmer on the ocean is worth the trip. But you have to watch the moon position. Tarpon always jump toward the moonlight. We've set baits on the opposite side of the boat from the moon and had tarpon jump over us so close you could see their scales!"

Another angler who catches lots of tarpon is Jerry Helms, who was the dock master at Bald Head Island Marina for 5 years until he accepted a position as the dock master at Saint James Plantation on the opposite side of the Cape Fear River.

"The tarpon fishing at Bald Head Island is as good as it gets anywhere," Helms said. "For good tarpon fishing, the water should

107

A hooked tarpon leaps from Pamlico Sound. A tarpon strike is one of the most exciting events for anglers who fish from king mackerel boats.

get hot early in the summer. You can look for the fish to show up in numbers as early as the first full moon in July."

Helms also anchors and fishes on the bottom. He prefers to fish late in the afternoon and early in the morning, although he sometimes sees tarpon feeding at the surface on moonlit nights.

"I fish with live crabs, dead menhaden or dead spots while chumming with menhaden ground up over the side with a commercial grinder," Helms said. "The best tide conditions for catching tarpon seem to occur from 2 hours after a low tide all the way through the flood tide."

Helms uses a 6-foot length of 130-pound monofilament leader with a 7/0 straight hook or a 10/0 or 11/0 circle hook. He uses a 100-pound swivel to tie the leader to a 25-pound test line. A plastic fish-finder sleeve slides on the line above the swivel and holds a sinker big enough to hold the bait on the bottom, usually 2 to 4 ounces. Helms' rods are lighter weight than Miller's and are 30-pound class, 7 1/2-foot king mackerel live-bait rods equipped with *Shimano* reels. Sometimes he also uses a *Corsair 400* baitcasting reel spooled with 14-pound test monofilament line.

With the lighter tackle, Helms usually has to chase the fish instead of fighting them from an anchored position. He ties the anchor to a floating anchor ball and uses a slipknot to tie the boat to the ball. When a fish strikes, he unties the boat and follows the fish.

"The key to fighting a tarpon is never to give the fish any slack," Helms said. "I fight a tarpon like a king mackerel, by pumping and reeling lightly. When a tarpon jumps I bow to the fish. They pull harder when jumping. That way you can give them some leeway to keep the line from breaking while still keeping contact. If you give a tarpon any slack, the hooks can pull. That's probably the main reason for missing a tarpon."

The hard bony plates in the mouth of a tarpon can translate into poor hook penetration. That's why Helms likes to use circle hooks.

"When you use circle hooks, you don't have to set them into the fish," Helms said. "I set the reel in free spool with the clicker on and let him move off about 30 seconds. He doesn't feel the pressure until you put the reel in gear. I fish with anywhere from 7 to 13 pounds of drag and the hook imbeds itself in the corner of the fish's mouth."

With the lighter tackle, Helms said it takes a long time to land a big fish. Fortunately, a hooked fish will usually run near the beach. When a fish runs into shallow water, it's easier for the angler because tarpon waste a lot of energy when they jump. If a tarpon gets into deep water it doesn't jump as much and it can take a couple of hours to land the fish. The downside of a fish that stays

This Pamlico Sound tarpon fight is nearly ended. A tarpon is considered "landed" once the leader touches the mate's hand.

in shallow water is it can swim inside the shoals where it's dangerous for an angler to follow. If a tarpon gets into the shoals, the angler's best option is to give up some line and keep up the pressure while waiting for the tarpon to turn back toward the boat.

"The water at the shoals goes from 20 feet to 0 feet in a very short horizontal distance," Helms said. "You have to be aware of where you're at at all times or you can run out of water."

When sea conditions are rough, Miller uses a spare life vest that has reflective tape sewed onto it as a channel marker. He anchors it in a slough with a safe water depth so he can find the return path for heading north to Wilmington through the Cape Fear River with a spotlight after it gets dark. On a calm night, he runs through the ocean to Carolina Beach Inlet to return home. But Helms doesn't usually fish through the night. Since he launches across the river at Southport, he has a shorter run home.

Another place besides the shoals where Helms catches tarpon is at Shell Bed Island. Following a route directly south of "The Rocks" at Fort Fisher on a map, an angler can locate Muddy Slough. Shell Bed Island is the island that separates Muddy Slough from Striking Island. There's a deep hole where the water depth increases from 3 feet to 32 feet at the west bank of Shell Bed Island where tarpon like to feed. Helms anchors on top of the sandbar in his 18-foot Scout boat named *Two's the Limit* and drops baits into the hole. Helms said the minimum-sized, center console style boat for fishing the area is 17 feet. He said the best fishing days are calm days, and although anglers in smaller aluminum johnboats have landed tarpon, he doesn't recommend such small craft because the river can become rough with little warning.

Tarpon are too bony to eat and are nearly always released alive. Tarpon are landed with gloved hands by grabbing the lower jaw. If the hook is set deep or in a location where it would endanger the angler to remove it, the leader is cut as near to the hook as possible or broken off by pulling against the weight of the fish. Otherwise the hook is removed with pliers and the tarpon revived if necessary by moving the fish back and forth in the water to help it pump oxygen through its gills before it's sent on its way.

Tarpon hooks should never be made of stainless steel. Hooks that will rust away quickly in a saltwater environment are the smart angler's choice because many fish escape by breaking the line.

Captain George Beckwith, Jr. operates *Down East Guide Service* and is one of the top tarpon-fishing guides in North Carolina. Beckwith's clients catch tarpon from Pamlico Sound and land as many as 200 in a single summer. Like the tarpon at Bald Head Island, Pamlico Sound tarpon also show up when the weather is hot, usually during July and August. While the fish at Bald Head Island are usually caught at night, Beckwith scouts the sound near Oriental to find tarpon during the day. Beckwith often climbs onto the T-top of his 23-foot Parker boat when scanning for fish.

"Calm days are best for finding tarpon," Beckwith said. "You can see schools of tarpon rolling at the surface when there's no wind. But a slight ripple on the water seems to make the fish bite better."

Once Beckwith finds a school of tarpon, he may troll a lure such as a *Rapala* or *Rat-L-Trap* as he approaches the fish. He sometimes hooks a fish with a lure while he studies the school.

"Just trying different things works sometimes," Beckwith said. "With tarpon, anything might work and nothing might work. You don't get that many chances so it pays to try everything. I've caught them with dead baits, live baits and lures."

Once he determines which direction a school of tarpon is heading, Beckwith navigates quietly and slowly ahead of the direction they seem to be moving, then anchors the boat a couple of hundred yards in front of the school. He casts cut chunks of croakers and spots from all four corners of the boat. He also tosses chunks of cut fish in all directions so the scent will attract feeding tarpon to the baited hooks.

Beckwith keeps several hundred yards between his boat and any other boats fishing the same school. A tarpon can run off 300 yards of line and tangle other anglers' fishing lines or anchor lines if they're nearby.

"I cover as large an area as possible with baits," Beckwith said. "Even though you see tarpon feeding on top, they prefer to strike a dead bait soaking on the bottom."

Beckwith fishes his baits on a 14/0 circle hook weighted with a 2-ounce egg sinker pegged to the leader. The leader consists of about 6 feet of double line tied with a *Bimini* twist, and 18 inches of 120-pound test monofilament tied to the double line by using a 150-pound barrel swivel. His rods are 7-foot *Cape Fear Rod* 20 to 30-pound class spinning rods mated with *Fin Nor* size 20 reels or *Diawa 6000* reels. The reels hold at least 160 yards of 30-pound test mono line.

When a tarpon strikes, the line may go slack if he's swimming toward the boat. But the most exciting strike is when the fish leaps from the water.

"The circle hooks sets itself," Beckwith said. "The sinker imbeds the hook in the corner of the jaws as the fish swims away. You just hold on and wear down the fish with the drag and you may adjust the drag setting several times during the fight depending upon what the fish is doing. You'll probably have to pull up the anchor to follow a big tarpon so you won't run out of line."

Beckwith said most tarpon are lost when they jump. Anglers who don't bow to the fish to release some line tension invite broken lines when a tarpon clears the water.

"If you keep the line tight when the fish jumps, he tends to fall back to the water facing toward you," Beckwith said. "If he falls back on the leader or the line, chances are it will break. Bowing releases enough line tension to allow the fish to fall away from you. Losing a tarpon after waiting for hours or days in the summer heat for a shot at one is tough. Breaking the line during a fight with a tarpon feels almost like breaking your heart. It's going to happen, though. All you can do is be happy you got to hook one up and seem him jump, then get set up and give it another try."

Additional Information

Captain George Beckwith, Jr. operates *Down East Guide Service* out of Oriental, specializing in big red drum as well as tarpon. Anglers can contact him at (252) 249-3101.

A barracuda is a fearsome fish and an awesome fighter when caught on light tackle.

Chapter 17

Blistered by Barracuda

I was relatively new to saltwater fishing when I was invited on an Atlantic foray for king mackerel by my fishing pal, Phil Pare. He had just finished overhauling and re-rigging a 20-foot Mako center console boat for offshore fishing and needed a copilot along for the test ride.

After spending a half-hour or so catching a livewell full of menhaden to use as bait, we motored 13 miles south of Masonboro Inlet to the Dredge Wreck, an artificial reef numbered AR-382.

The ride out was pleasant despite the August heat. We ran a heading of 160 degrees from Masonboro Inlet. The day was calm and the water slick. It was still early in the day when we arrived at the marker buoy about 30 minutes after passing the sea buoy at Masonboro Inlet.

There was no electronic navigation equipment onboard, since a Loran unit was an expensive option back in those days. Like most nearshore reefs, the Dredge Wreck was easy to find on the calm sea by compass heading alone.

Removing a pair of king mackerel live bait rods from the rocket launcher rod holders on the side of the console and heading back to the stern to set them off the boat's rear corners, I passed the opaque livewell tank set in the center of the deck in front of the motor. I noticed the baits stacked like sardines on the bottom of the tank.

"Uh-oh. Looks like we've got problems," I said. "I hope you have some frozen baits in the cooler."

Pare glanced at the tank full of dead menhaden. Switching the pump on and off did no good because the motor was as dead as the bait. It turned out that a fuse had blown because of a short circuit in the well-used livewell pump motor. I vowed right then never to head offshore without a spare livewell pump onboard and to periodically check live baits on the way out to a fishing hole. But the self-promise to have a redundant system in the future certainly did no good on that particular day.

Pare said a bad word or two. Then he started rummaging around in his tackle box.

"There's Spanish mackerel jumping all around," Pare said. "Let's try for a few of them so we won't have wasted a trip."

Trolling around the buoy, we quickly hooked up a 16-inch Spanish mackerel on a *Clarkspoon*. However, less than half the fish came to the boat. Not much more than the head of the fish dangled from the hook when we reeled in the line.

"Barracuda," Pare said in disgust as he eyed the worthless remains of the Spanish mackerel.

We continued to troll as the barracuda had a feast, neatly snipping all of the Spanish mackerel we hooked just behind the gills.

"Well, if we can't catch any king mackerel, we might just as well have some fun," Pare said.

He tied a small jig onto the line of a spinning rod and made a very short cast into a jumping school of Spanish mackerel. Locking down the drag, he wind-milled the reel handle and got the fish into the boat just in time to avoid the snap of a barracuda's teeth.

He dumped the fish into the "dead" well and dumped in a bucket full of fresh seawater to liven it back up with some oxygen.

"Check this out," he said.

I put on the polarized sunglasses he took off and handed to me. Looking down into the water where his finger pointed beneath the buoy, I could see several dozen barracuda suspended along the cable that held the buoy at anchor. It was no wonder we couldn't get any Spanish mackerel to the boat while trolling long lines near the buoy.

After tying a king mackerel live bait rig onto one of the trolling rods, Pare retrieved the wriggling Spanish mackerel from the livewell and hooked the leading treble hook into its nose. A second treble hook dangled free alongside the fish.

He handed me the rod and instructed me to cast to the Spanish mackerel beneath the shadow of the buoy and leave the reel out of gear while the bait sank below the surface. I gave him back his sunglasses and did as instructed. Pare put on the sunglasses and watched the bait as it was attacked by the wolf pack guarding the buoy.

"He has it! Set the hook!" Pare shouted.

So quick was the strike that I couldn't feel the teeth of the barracuda slicing through the Spanish mackerel. I couldn't see the strike without the help of polarized sunglasses, but when Pare shouted, I turned the reel handle to engage the gears and hauled back on the rod. Instinctively, I had kept my thumb on the reel spool as I set the hook. What a mistake that was!

The fish cleared the water in a leap as high as the T-top, gnashing its teeth in an attempt to throw the hooks. As it hit the water, line ripped from the reel. My thumb was only against the spool for an instant, but the blister the line friction raised on the pad of my thumb was the size of a grape, and was destined to cause problems with casting for over a week. The memory of the pain served as a perpetual reminder of the incredible velocity of the barracuda's strike.

At the time, the blister didn't hurt at all as I concentrated on playing the fish. I merely held on while it melted the line from the reel. The speed and power of the fish was only exceeded by the height of his leaps. That barracuda was more fun to catch than any king mackerel and he lived up to his reputation as a game fish, even if he wasn't the intended target of the trip.

Between the fish's runs and jumps, I reeled and pumped. When he tired enough to be coaxed near the boat, Pare deftly reached down and unhooked the fish with long-nosed pliers. We laughed like kids at the fish's antics. Then we had a ball catching barracuda

Chris Foster, of *Yeah Right Charters* in Southport landed this big barracuda near an artificial reef

on Spanish mackerel and whole dead menhaden baits for the rest of the morning before we headed back to shore to replace the livewell pump.

Bane of the king mackerel angler, the great barracuda can slice a tournament-winning fish in two with a single pass and can part lines, destroy lures and wreck carefully-crafted live bait rigs in the flash of a scale. Citation-sized Spanish mackerel are no match for its stiletto teeth. Showing up in numbers when the water turns hot in mid- to late summer barracuda are legendary fighters. Most anglers despise them because of the damage they do to baits intended for other game fish, as well as the game fish themselves. They have a nasty habit of waiting until a hooked fish begins to tire before moving in for the easy meal, and the act of stealing fish meant for the table or the tournament scales does not endear them to fishermen.

Barracuda can show up anywhere in ocean waters, from just outside the beaches on out to the Gulf Stream. While most anglers avoid waters once they become infested with barracuda, those who want the fastest action with fins, or who are having trouble finding other game fish in hot weather, won't hook a gamier fish than a 'cuda. Besides live and natural baits, barracuda readily strike jigs, spoons, topwater poppers, lures and flies. Large flashy baits and lures, or lures that make lots of surface commotion work best for catching fearless barracuda. They can be landed on any type of tackle that has the line capacity to stop their long first run, bearing in mind that a 200 yard run is not unusual for a large barracuda when hooked on light tackle.

While the fish is edible, most anglers avoid eating barracuda. They have a pungent odor all their own and most captains won't bring one aboard and place it in the fish box because the scent lasts all day and is unpleasant to most fishermen.

The best way to release a barracuda is by protecting the hand with a glove and snipping the leader near the fish with wire cutters.

A long de-hooking tool can also be used to free a lightly-hooked fish. Anglers must use extreme caution when releasing barracuda and keep handling to a minimum because the teeth that are so formidable for slicing fish flesh can cause severe damage to a human hand. Grabbing the leader while the fish's head is pointed upward toward the angler puts the fish in a dangerous position if it makes a last feeble leap beside the boat. It's prudent to keep the body of the fish parallel to the water as the fish is released.

Ciguatera and Barracuda

Dr. Peter Meyer is an emergency medicine physician with expertise regarding hazardous marine animals. He is also author of *Nature Guide to the Carolina Coast* and *Blue Crabs: Catch 'em, Cook 'em, Eat 'em.*

Meyer said, "I very much like the taste of barracuda. It's not as oily as king and tastes more like Spanish. But not many people bring them in because of rumors of ciguatera.

"If you look at worldwide statistics, ciguatera is a huge problem. It's the most common cause of fish-related illness in the world.

"The toxin concentrates in predatory fish as it goes up the food chain. Over 400 species have been documented with ciguatera. The most common species are reef fish like snapper, grouper, barracuda and sea bass.

"Ciguatera is caused by a dinoflagellate that secretes the toxin as it enters the base of the food chain at the zooplankton level. The toxin is concentrated in the higher predators through the eating of forage species.

"If the fish lives in local waters, there should be no problem because the toxin only occurs in tropical waters. Barracuda migrate, just like dolphin and wahoo. However, there was one ciguatera episode documented in 1987 in North Carolina.

"Ten people were affected. Symptoms were vomiting, diarrhea and cramps, along with burning, tingling and numbness and a reversal of temperature sensation—where things that should've felt hot felt cold and things that should've felt cold, felt hot.

"The people ate the barracuda as appetizers the day after it was caught without symptoms. When they ate thick barracuda steaks a week later, they developed ciguatera. Cooking and freezing do not remove the toxin.

"The fish was caught off the western edge of the Gulf Stream at the mid-North Carolina coast. It's almost certain the fish migrated from the Caribbean.

"There's risk in eating anything, but the chances of contracting ciguatera are very small. To put it in perspective, there's a greater risk of dying from eating a hamburger than from eating a barracuda."

Jerry Dilsaver with his 1998 USAA Angler of the Year trophy and jacket.

Chapter 18

King Mackerel Tournament Tips

Catching huge, smoker kings is always tough with any gear. The speed of a 40-pound king mackerel at the strike is so incredible that many inexperienced anglers make the mistake of cranking up the drag to try to prevent the fish from making off with an entire spool of line.

Commercial and recreational anglers catch lots of small to average-sized kings using heavy trolling gear, but the tournament-winning fish are nearly always lured to the scales by a live bait dancing at the end of a line as thin a spider silk.

Live bait and tournament fishing go hand in hand; it was the discovery of the "slow-trolling" technique by anglers along the North Carolina coast that began the quest for catching big kings on light sporting gear.

Kenny McGee of Wrightsville Beach, North Carolina, said, "We got the idea from pier anglers in the early 1970s. Pier anglers had used multiple hook rigs for some time. They slid the bait to the water on a trolley line anchored from a second rod and used a float to keep the bait near the surface. We decided that if we could catch baits, keep them alive, and troll them behind a boat, we could go to the fish instead of having to wait for them to come to us on a pier.

"Livewells and cast nets were unheard of. We snagged menhaden right in the ocean, using treble hooks cast on spinning gear. Jerking the hooks through a school of menhaden would give us live fish to set out on pier king rigs right over the side.

"It worked so well that anglers began using coolers with pumps rigged to them to pump in fresh water and keep menhaden alive. Then cast nets began to be used to catch baits by the dozens."

Today, livewells are standard equipment in boats specifically designed for king mackerel fishing. The slow-trolling technique worked so well that the sport caught fire, initiating the "my fish is bigger than your fish" camaraderie that led to friendly, fishing club competitions, and then to full-scale tournaments that are the saltwater angler's equivalent of freshwater bass tournaments.

Centered in the Carolinas, but with counterparts from Mississippi to Virginia, there are around 60 tournaments sanctioned by organizations like the Southern Kingfish Association (SKA) and U.S. Anglers Association (USAA). The competition is fierce for a total purse that exceeds 2.5 million dollars, and that isn't including the dozens of club and town-sponsored tournaments that are held to raise a little cash for volunteer fire departments and other worthy local causes.

The tournament craze has spawned keen interest. While weekend fishermen won the early tournaments and took home nothing but some fishing gear and bragging rights, modern competitions and the lure of cash have spawned professional king mackerel anglers.

One of the best professional king mackerel anglers is Jerry Dilsaver, of Long Beach, North Carolina. Consistently finishing in the "top ten" aboard several boats that have carried the named *Carolina Adventure* and *North Carolina Sportsman* for years, Dilsaver won the 1998 USAA trophy for angler of the year by accumulating more pounds of tournament-caught king mackerel than any other angler in the 700-member organization. In 2001, he won the SKA National Championship for boats 23 feet and under. A true professional, Dilsaver makes a living by weighing in huge fish and by teaching dozens of annual seminars on how he catches them. He has fished in as many as 24 tournaments in a single year, and he teaches schools for anglers more than 70 days a year.

"Over the years, we have gone to lighter and lighter tackle," Dilsaver said. "Big fish aren't easy to fool. The proper use of light tackle lets the baits swim in a natural manner, resulting in more strikes from large fish."

Dilsaver says his crews nearly mutinied when he began using lighter and lighter lines. He descended down the line-class categories through 25-, 20-, 17-, and finally 15-pound test monofilament lines that were spooled onto his conventional, revolving spool reels. But the proof in the sub-weight lines became evident at the scales.

"I use 7-foot, medium action rods with reels that hold 450 yards of 15-pound test, high-visibility monofilament line," Dilsaver said. "The reels I like come equipped with level wind line guides, but I remove them. No manufactured level wind device will work smoothly and quickly enough to prevent jams and the broken lines that result when a big king mackerel strikes. The fish are simply too fast. The typical tournament-winning fish will weigh above 40 pounds. In the spring, a fish that size will run long and hard, taking about 300 yards of line. In summer, when the water temperature is hot, a big fish will run as hard, but will become exhausted after 200 yards. In fall, it's not unusual for the same size fish to take 400 yards of line before stopping his first run."

The best way to judge the size of a king mackerel is by the duration of the run. A king's run lasts about 1 second per pound. That's a good way to tell if a tournament winner is on the end of the line.

Water temperature and dissolved oxygen are the factors that affect the endurance of the fish. At ideal king mackerel temperatures of around 70 degrees, water provides higher dissolved oxygen content than water that has warmed to 80 degrees. Like a sprinter, a fish "hits the wall" and stops when he can't get enough oxygen to fuel his run.

When a fish strikes, the downriggers come up immediately on Dilsaver's boat. Once the fish takes a heading away from the boat, the top lines are reeled in, except for a single line that's kept baited and in the water. The angler moves with the rod to the bow, and the captain chases the fish with the boat to regain line, always keeping the rod tip in sight to judge the direction and distance to the fish by the angle the line departs from the rod tip.

Communication between the captain and angler is imperative. The angler must tell the boat operator when to slow or stop the boat to avoid creating any slack in the line, which will result in a lost fish because the hooks simply fall out.

"If we're lucky, the fish tires in about 10 minutes," Dilsaver said. "If he's sufficiently stunned, he can usually be led to the boat by smoothly turning the reel handle. Pumping the rod often alarms the fish and really doesn't regain line fast enough. When pumping and reeling, you can lose as much line as you regain each time you lower the rod tip. I run my drag tension just heavy enough to keep the bait from taking line, then bump it up to 3 or 4 pounds after the fish stops the first time.

"As the fish comes up, the angler says, 'I see color,' which means he sees the flash of the fish. The gaff man moves behind the angler and watches over his shoulder. The gaff goes into the water when the leader emerges above the surface. If the fish is struck when it's deeper in the water, light refraction distorts the angle and can result in a missed fish. I use a 12-foot gaff with a 2-inch hook. Some anglers are astonished that the small hook will hold, but a world-record king of 79 pounds was boated with a 2-inch hook. The key is to come over the top of the fish and penetrate the back at the center balance point of the fish. The bones of the dorsal fin at that point will hold the hook solidly. Also, the fish will bleed very little when struck there, keeping him from losing fluid and weight."

If the fish is missed or won't come to the boat on the first run, the battle continues. The second run tends to be about half the length of the first. There's nothing an angler can do except give chase to regain line and allow the drag to tire the fish. The fish is capable of making multiple runs before coming alongside.

However, the longer the fish is in the water, the more likely it is that a barracuda or shark will attack the king mackerel, leaving the angler with nothing more than fish lips to reel in. The upside is that the commotion can also attract a large king, which will hit the remaining bait trolling behind the boat. With a feisty fish, the give-and-take of line can go on for as long as 45 to 90 minutes before he comes within range of the gaff.

When gaffed, the fish is worked into an in-deck box filled with ice and the leader is removed from the line. If the fish is a potential winner, the hooks are removed once he settles down and he's put in a special plastic fish bag filled with ice. The bag is then compressed to remove as much air as possible and prevent dehydration.

"I've won tournaments by hundredths of an ounce," Dilsaver said. "I've beaten anglers with larger kings who didn't care properly for a fish that may have lost as much as 10 percent of its live weight prior to weigh-in."

The hooks sometimes fall out as the fish is swung over the side. Ideally, hooks find the inside of the mouth and lodge into hard bone, but many times they get stuck in the skin of the side or in a fin. Two 4x strong hooks in No. 6 size, connected by 5 inches of No. 4, coffee-colored, stainless steel, single-strand wire make up Dilsaver's live bait rig. The front hook is tied to a 5-foot leader of No. 3 single-strand wire with a No. 10 swivel providing the connection to the line. The wire is tied using a combination of three haywire twists and five barrel wraps. This rig is the key to light tackle, live-bait fishing.

The preferred bait of most tournament anglers is menhaden, a species that's a major forage fish for kings. Other potential baits are mullets, pinfish, cigar minnows, herring, sardines and shad. In fact, when fishing offshore, almost any species of reef fish can be caught on *Sabiki* rigs, which are multiple-hook rigs with feather jigs that are dropped near hard bottom areas or other structure. By jigging them up and down anglers can catch lots of small baitfish quickly.

127

Richard Denning, Jerry Dilsaver and Bob Black with the 40-pound king mackerel that sealed the 2001 SKA National Championship. Photo by Sam White, courtesy of SKA.

The bait is hooked sideways through the nostrils with the front hook. The trailing hook is stuck into the fish near the vent.

The proper speed to troll is just fast enough to keep the bait from out-swimming the boat. If the rod tip bends continuously, it indicates the bait is being pulled through the water. A bait that is pulled along will die quickly and doesn't appear as natural to a king mackerel as a bait that swims freely.

Dilsaver adds a skirt in front of the bait in three situations: when others are catching fish with them; when he wants to make a smaller bait look larger; and when fishing dirty water. Preferred colors are light, such as pink, yellow, white and chartreuse. The important thing is keeping the skirt far enough in front of the bait by using a bead or swivel to keep it away from the gills, which reduce its liveliness.

Clear water calls for refining the leader to a 9-inch length of No. 4 wire and a 4 1/2-foot length of low-visibility, 30-pound monofilament leader tied together with an *Albright* knot. Less metal translates into less likelihood that the fish will sense the leader and avoid the bait.

The flow of fresh water through the livewell must be constant. In order to keep oxygen evenly distributed in the tank, water should enter the bottom and flow in a circular motion to the top of the tank before discharging. Re-circulating tanks won't keep menhaden alive due to an enzyme the fish release that depletes the water's oxygen level. Also, menhaden and mullet are filter feeders that constantly take nourishment from the plankton in the water. Without fresh water, they starve. When placing a bait in the livewell, a cast net full is usually way too many. One bait per gallon of tank capacity in water that has a temperature of about 70 degrees is a good rule of thumb, and fewer than that as the water temperature approaches 80 degrees.

Dilsaver uses a six-rod spread, and it takes planning to prevent tangles with that many rods. Line No. 1 is set long from the starboard side overhead the T-top holder. Length varies from 100 feet when fishing in a crowd of boats to as long as 100 yards in open water. Line No. 2 is set three-fourths the length of line No. 1 from the port side T-top holder. Line No. 3 is set 30 to 50 feet behind the boat on the port side downrigger release clip at two-thirds the distance to the bottom. Line No. 4 is set 20 feet behind the boat on the starboard side downrigger at one-third the distance to the bottom. Line No. 5 is set from a transom rod holder at 40 to 50 feet behind the boat. Line No. 6 is set at 15 feet behind the boat from a transom rod holder. When shutting down one motor and trolling with the other, the longer transom line is set behind the prop wash to keep the bait out of the turbulence, while the other is set beside the prop wash.

Sometimes the individual baits will swim toward the center of the spread, in which case they must be switched with their counterpart on the opposite side of the boat. Baits must be watched constantly to avoid tangles. Setting the longer lines out first and working to the shorter lines prevents tangles by keeping the baits from passing one another as line is let out. It takes a crew of three anglers to consistently keep all of the baits in the water and to maneuver the boat, play and gaff a king mackerel.

While these tactics work for a tournament professional, they also serve as a guide for the weekend angler who just wants to boat a limit of king mackerel. Weekenders can use fewer lines, heavier tackle, frozen baits and more colorful skirts to draw strikes from average-sized kings, smaller "snakes" and the occasional big "smokers." But when thousands of dollars are at stake, you can bet that the heaviest king mackerel will be brought to the weigh-in by the angler who goes the lightest on his tackle and keeps the most baits in the water for the longest length of time.

Chapter 19

Fooling Kings With Artificial Lures

Slow-trolling a live menhaden has become the accepted way to catch a king mackerel on light tackle. But it wasn't all that long ago that most king mackerel were caught by anglers who used lures.

Using lures for king mackerel involved fast-trolling methods. Speed is what gave *Drone Spoons* and cedar plugs their lifelike wriggle and dance. Trolling such lures successfully also required heavy tackle and the larger spoons required planers to take them down to the fish, killing the fight when an otherwise sporty fish was hooked. While many offshore charter captains and commercial fishermen continue to use fast-trolling methods, slow-trolling is still the bastion of sport fishermen.

Tim Barefoot is a Wilmington angler who has always had a passion for fishing. He operates *No Shoes Charters* and fishes from a 25-foot Sea Cat, a catamaran that provides a stable platform, even in rough seas. These days, however, he is more likely to be seen at promotional events than charter fishing. Through dedication and hard work, he has seen the dream of creating an artificial lure that kings readily mistake for natural prey become reality. Word of the success of his lures is taking the nation's fishing waters by storm. On the great lakes, his lures are taking huge lake trout, and in the nation's rivers, salmon are eating them like candy. But it was the desire to catch big king mackerel that gave him inspiration.

"The good thing about using lures is that they live forever in your tackle box," Barefoot said. "It never hurts to have a box of

Captain Tim Barefoot of *No Shoes Charters* in Wilmington heads offshore for a day of trolling for king mackerel with one of his *Cha-Raider* lures ready for action.

frozen baits or ballyhoos when heading out for a day of king mackerel fishing. But catching live baits with a cast net burns a lot of fishing time. I like to be fishing at first light, not trying to catch bait with a dozen other boats circling around, scattering the schools of menhaden and driving them deep."

132

Barefoot admits that his lures will probably not out-fish live menhaden for tournament fishing. However, for day-to-day angling situations they give an angler a great alternative.

"Most anglers use frozen baits these days," Barefoot said. "But a *Cha-Raider* will catch more fish than a frozen cigar minnow every time because it actually swims while a frozen bait just drags through the water."

Barefoot Baits' Cha-Raider is a lure cast of solid Nylon, with a one-piece wiring harness and a lead keel molded into the lure. The lure is painted in realistic colors; the cigar minnow model, which has a gold/green back and white belly is the best inshore pattern, and the herring pattern is best for offshore fishing.

"You have to match the color of the bait to what the fish are eating," Barefoot said. "Cigar minnows and herring are a king mackerel's favorite prey. Size is important and the lure should be the same size as the baitfish in the same area. The 5-inch or 7-inch model is great for slow-trolling for king mackerel. When you're blue-water fishing for dolphin, tuna and wahoo, it's better to go with the 8-inch or 10-inch size and use a blue mackerel, red and black or dorado color pattern."

Barefoot is a mold maker by training and operates an industrial maintenance business. He developed his initial lure molds from the actual bodies of cigar minnows and Boston mackerel.

"I went out and caught baitfish and created the molds around them," Barefoot said. "But they didn't swim properly. I had to thin the bodies to get the action I wanted."

Barefoot spent many years fishing commercially with some great captains. He spent hours at night watching the behavior of baitfish and predatory fish beneath the glow of lights.

"I watched giant schools of cigar minnows under the lights at night," Barefoot said. "It's the fish that swims erratically that predators always eat. A baitfish will dart from a school. He is injured, sick or weak. Predators move in to take advantage of the easy meal."

Barefoot's catamaran was docked in a distant location the day

Tim Barefoot of *No Shoes Charters* in Wilmington uses a downrigger to take lures deep and to keep them spread apart to prevent tangles.

we set out for king mackerel, so we fished with one of his lifelong fishing companions, Jimmy Mintz, from his 28-foot Mako. Onboard was Taylor, Barefoot's 9-year-old son, who fishes with his dad every time he gets a chance.

We arrived at the Dredge Wreck, located about 10 miles off Carolina Beach, before the sun had completely awakened. Since we didn't have to chase live baits at dawn, we arrived long before other anglers could create a crowd.

"You can troll *Cha-Raiders* at the same speed as live baits," Barefoot said. "Although they remain stable and fish well up to 7 1/2 knots, they're ideally suited to slow-trolling speeds of 1 1/2 to 2 1/2 knots. Anglers can mix them in the spread with live or frozen baits and give the fish another choice. However, I like to fish six or eight rods with similar lures in a tight pattern. It imitates the commotion of a school of baitfish and I think it brings in kings from longer distances."

The key to slow-trolling with lures is setting them in a pattern that keeps them from tangling or interfering with one another. Barefoot set the longest line from a transom rod holder at a distance of about 75 feet behind the boat. Another line was set from the transom inside the long line and right in the prop wash of the motors.

"Watch the lure swim from side to side in the prop wash," Barefoot said. "It matches the action of an injured baitfish because it doesn't swim in a straight line."

Indeed, the lure fluttered just beneath the surface and swam at an angle until it hit the "wall" of the prop wash on one side of the boat. Then it reversed direction and swam all the way across the prop wash created by both motors until it hit the wall of the other side, then repeated its course. The action is absolutely maddening to king mackerel, who pound the lure as it imitates the sideways motion of the injured fish Barefoot saw under the lights.

"The long line will run at a depth of about 15 feet," Barefoot said. "For deeper trolling, we set the lures from a downrigger."

A pair of downriggers was used to take two *Cha-Raiders* to two different depths below the long line's depth. One was set 10 to 15 feet above the bottom and the other split the difference between the long line and the bottom line. A pair of outriggers was used to set a line from each side of the boat's T-top. The downrigger lines and outrigger lines were set with about 15 to 20 feet of line extending beyond the release clips.

"There's very little drag on the rod with these lures," Barefoot said. "You can fish them on everyday, king mackerel 20-pound class tackle. But I like my rods a little stiffer, so I cut the top 4 inches from live bait rods. This not only makes a better trolling rod, it also gives the rod more backbone when using lures for casting or jigging. The beauty of *Cha-Raiders* is that they're just as deadly when you drift or anchor up and jig, or when you cast them to a school of fish, as when they're trolled."

When he fishes a ledge, Barefoot said he doesn't like to stay right on top of it and run his sonar. He feels that the fish will not stay inside the sound cone. He also thinks that big kings don't particularly like the sound of a running motor.

"It's better to find the ledge with a color scope, then drop some marker buoys to show the location," Barefoot said. "By using a compass and the marker buoys as a guide, you can shut off the depthfinder and the motors and cast to the ledge, letting the lure fall to within 5 to 10 feet of the bottom. Jigging the *Cha-Raider* lure up and down will catch anything that's there. Grouper love them and any king mackerel will hit the lure on the way up. Amberjacks are keen-eyed fish and the fact that they'll instantly attack a *Cha-Raider* tells me that they think they're real prey fish. The secret is in the vibration. The lure is retrieved in short bursts. You can feel the lure through about a dozen vibrations when you're jigging it properly."

Besides a stiffer rod, Barefoot uses other tackle that is different from what most live-bait anglers use. While his reels are standard *Diawa* reels, they're spooled with yellow, 50-pound superbraid lines. The last 5 feet of line is colored with a red permanent marker, which Barefoot said makes the braided line invisible in the water. Six to 10 feet of 30-pound fluorocarbon leader is tied to the superbraid using a jam knot, creating a wind-on leader. The tag ends of the lines are burned into blobs with a cigarette lighter as a precaution against knot slippage. The fluorocarbon is tied to a 10-inch length of No. 6 stainless steel wire with an *Albright* knot, and the wire tied to the lure eye using haywire twists and barrel wraps.

As we trolled in figure eights around the structure, a dive boat and other anglers began to show up. While other anglers fishing live baits had to travel wide trolling courses, Mintz was able to navigate his boat in tight turns and stay right inside the strike zone.

While we trolled, Barefoot discussed the advantages of using lures to catch kings.

"Using lures saves fishing time and lots of mess and fuss over using live baits," Barefoot said. "There's also a cost factor with live baits. You have cast nets, livewells and pumps that cause additional battery wear. Chasing bait burns up fuel and time when you could be fishing. With frozen baits the cost factor is $15 for a box of cigar minnows, which you'll use up in a single day. If bluefish, sharks or barracuda attack, they use up baits even faster.

A 5-inch *Cha-Raider* costs $14.50 and a 7-incher costs $18.50, and it lasts forever. In the long run, it's more economical to use lures to catch kings."

When he's slow-trolling, Barefoot sets his drags at 4 to 6 pounds of tension, which allows a king to set the hook itself. He doesn't adjust the drag during the fight; he leaves it alone until the fish is brought to the gaff.

"If you play a king mackerel on a tight drag, they can pull the hooks free, even with artificial lures," Barefoot said. "You want to keep the same tension on him. If he stayed hooked during his fast runs, he'll stay hooked at the same tension when he's at the side of the boat."

When he's drifting a ledge and jigging, Barefoot uses a tighter drag tension. He begins with about 10 pounds and adjusts it to a lower setting when a king strikes.

"With grouper, you have to use the heavier drag to get them off a reef," Barefoot said. "You can tell when a king mackerel hits because he runs so fast. You just adjust the drag down to 4 to 6 pounds and let him wear himself out."

I asked Barefoot if there was any other place he liked to catch big king mackerel and he named two of his other hot spots.

"Besides the Dredge Wreck, I like to fish 23-Mile Rock and WR-4," Barefoot said. "They're all different distances and fishing them depends upon the sea conditions. The Dredge Wreck is the closest and it's a quick run back to the inlet if seas get sloppy, while WR-4 is great on calmer days."

For grouper, Barefoot has secret spots in the same areas. He winked when he was about to tell me the location of "Taylor's Secret Hole."

"No, Daddy. Don't tell that one!" Taylor said.

Barefoot smiled and said, "Let's just say it's about 23 miles off the hill."

Additional Information

Captain Tim Barefoot operates *No Shoes Charters* out of Wrightsville Beach. Anglers can contact him at (910) 392-1683.

Captain Fisher Culbreth of *Capture Charters* in Carolina Beach caught this "chopper" bluefish with a topwater popper.

Chapter 20

Seeking Snapper and Chopper Bluefish

Where and when and why huge "chopper" bluefish have disappeared and will reappear has always been a mystery. Perhaps the incredibly ravenous schools of big bluefish migrate farther offshore than where most anglers concentrate their efforts at catching them. Or, it may be that their numbers have actually remained fairly high throughout their range and it's just a lack of angler catch data that creates a misconception of under-abundance. It could even be that their numbers are naturally cyclic.

The fish are highly migratory and can swim from Maine to Florida in a single year. Such fast-moving fish create problems for fishery managers who may never find answers to sport anglers' questions.

In spite of their mysterious nature, there always seems to be enough "chopper" bluefish of above 8 pounds in North Carolina's coastal waters to make fishing interesting whenever large schools of smaller yearling fish called "snappers" make their showing. Some offshore anglers curse big chopper bluefish when they run across them if they're after other species because of the way they kink up wire leaders, cut mono leaders and destroy anything less than the sturdiest of lures. This destructive nature becomes even more annoying with live baits; a school of choppers can eat the entire contents of a livewell full of big menhaden intended for catching king mackerel in a matter of minutes.

Whether he considers bluefish the blessing or the curse of the Atlantic Ocean, no angler can cast doubt on the sporting qualities of bluefish. They leap like miniature tarpon. While airborne their teeth gnash at leaders, hooks and lures and their gill plates clatter, creating an ominous rattle like nightmarish castanets. The sound of hooked bluefish clearing the water can send chills up and down an angler's spine because the teeth making that racket are sharp enough to slice off fingers. In the speed and endurance department, they have few peers when hooked on light tackle, and make multiple, streaking runs before tiring enough to come to the boat.

Rick Caton, captain of the *Free Agent* out of *Oregon Inlet Fishing Center*, said that he primarily targets smaller snapper bluefish for his clients.

"I catch the little ones along the beach and back in the sound up in the Old House Channel behind Oregon Inlet by trolling," said Caton. "The Old House Channel is actually part of the Intracoastal Waterway. Along the beach, I catch fish just behind the inlet bar in shallow water."

Caton trolls two No. 1 planers on a pair of planer rods and on a second pair of planer rods, he trolls with two trolling sinkers. One sinker weighs 4 ounces and one sinker weighs 2 ounces to carry the lures to different depths.

The lines from the two rods with the planers are set close to the boat. The line from the rod with the 4-ounce trolling weight is set 100 feet behind the boat and the line from the rod with the 2-ounce trolling weight is set 150 feet behind the boat. By varying the distances and depths of the lures, Caton quickly finds the schools and keeps his clients in the fish.

He trolls a two-lure rig consisting of a 1/8-ounce *Sea Witch* trolling head with a long shank No. 2 or No. 3 hook. The hook must be straight to prevent spinning, and if he uses an offset hook, he uses pliers to turn the bend and align it with the shank.

The *Sea Witch* is tied 13 feet behind the planer or trolling weight on 80-pound monofilament leader by using a dropper loop. One leg of the dropper loop is clipped, leaving the other leg to act as a leader of about 5 inches when tied to the *Sea Witch*. Two and one-half feet behind the *Sea Witch* is tied a No. 0 or No. 1

Clarkspoon, although sometimes a white bucktail jig is used at the end of the rig. Colors for the *Sea Witch* or the bucktail jig are white or chartreuse. The *Sea Witch* is trimmed to act more like a jig than a skirt and is run with the fibers straight, rather than reversed as most anglers do, to make the skirt open like an umbrella. The extra action of the reversed skirt is not necessary for catching greedy bluefish.

If the fish won't hit this rig, Caton uses the same rig tied with 50-pound monofilament. The lighter leader attracts more strikes from snapper bluefish, but may be cut if a chopper bluefish hits.

"I look for baitfish with a color machine when the bluefish are deep," Caton said. "Where you find the bait, you can troll at that same depth and catch bluefish. If I see pelicans diving and menhaden schooling right up to the beach, or see the sprat minnows jumping, I know the bluefish are there."

The *Free Agent* is a 42-foot custom-built Harkers Island Boat with a tower, shade top and curtains. Caton also sight-fishes for cobia and stripers in shallow water. However, the waves can get really rough when Caton's trying to stay on top of a school of bluefish in the shallow water near the beach. Keeping a boat aligned for trolling in a zone with little bottom clearance and lots of wave action is what he terms "combat fishing." In spite of a chilly day, fighting to stay on the fish can cause him to sweat in near-freezing temperatures. As an alternative boat for fishing inside the sound on windy days, he often uses his 18-foot Downeaster center console boat, *Iron Will*.

For jigging over offshore reefs, Caton uses a two-hook "speck" rig. He cuts the pair of jigs off a commercial rig made for catching speckled trout and ties the rig back using 50-pound mono. This rig also works for trolling when the fish are finicky, or for jigging when a school of bluefish is located in a tight place.

T.W.'s Bait and Tackle in Kitty Hawk is located in the heart of bluefish territory. The owner, Terry Stewart, also has bait and tackle shops in Nag's Head and Corolla.

"Fishing for bluefish is always good near the Avalon and Kitty

Hawk Piers," said Stewart. "The best lures for casting to surfacing fish on spinning rods are jerk baits like *Got-cha's*."

The best conditions to fish are the incoming tide, with clear water and a light northeast wind, according to Stewart.

"Bluefish are sight-feeding fish that see well in good, clean water," said Stewart. "If the water's very clear, and fish are spotted or anglers are catching them consistently, trolling a *Hopkins* No. 150 or 225 spoon works very well for catching them."

For trolling in and near Oregon Inlet, the best lure for big chopper bluefish is a *Drone Spoon*, according to Stewart. The best colors are chrome and pink. For access to Oregon Inlet, there's a ramp on the southern tip of Bodie Island at the *Oregon Inlet Fishing Center.*

Stewart said that while there have always been lots of small bluefish, the big ones, if they do show up, arrive in late November or early December. The smaller fish weigh 1 to 3 pounds and the bigger ones weigh 12 to 20 pounds.

As some encouragement to anglers lamenting the lack of big blues, there were reports of some good runs of choppers weighing from 8 to 14 pounds beginning in the spring of 2000 along the southern coast. Biologists pointed to a successful federal management plan as the source of this apparent surge of big fish. They feel strongly that the numbers of choppers seen in the past will return by the year 2007 when their statistics say bluefish will have fully recovered from recreational over-fishing during the 1980s.

Ten miles offshore, boats were reporting catching all the choppers they could handle on king mackerel rigs with live bait. Along Topsail, Kure, and Carolina beaches anglers reported catching big bluefish from the surf by casting spoons, jigs and natural baits. The frenzies have lasted about three weeks during May. Anglers who appreciate chopper bluefish for the great game fish they truly are will be holding their breath, hoping fishery managers are right in their assessment. Hopefully the choppers have returned and will continue to show up without vanishing mysteriously once again.

Additional Information

Captain Rick Caton operates *Custom Sound Charters* out of Manteo. Anglers can contact him at (252) 473-1209.

Justin Marsh caught this false albacore or "spotted bonito" with fly tackle.

Chapter 21

Spotted or Striped, Bonito Offer Lots of Fun

Common names used to describe the same fish vary from one region of the country to another. Unfortunately for saltwater fishermen, common names can lead to confusion when describing the many different species that anglers can encounter on any given day.

Saltwater anglers' everyday names for the false albacore and Atlantic bonito are often interchanged across their range. These species are also collectively called "little tunny," "little tuna," "Boston mackerel" and "cerro mackerel." Atlantic bonito are also called "striped apes," while false albacore are also named "Fat Alberts" for their tenacious fighting abilities.

Perhaps the nicknames that best distinguish the two speedsters are the "striped bonito" for the Atlantic bonito and "spotted bonito" for the false albacore. Horizontal black stripes on the steel-blue back and flanks identify a fish as the Atlantic or striped bonito. Irregular black swirls mark the back and black spots dot the sides of the false albacore or spotted bonito. These two fish can readily be told apart from one another, so fishermen across the Atlantic should be able to tell which species they're catching when bragging about a memorable trip to their friends.

Fortunately, scientists avoid all this confusion with common names by designating the Atlantic bonito *Sarda sarda* and the false albacore *Euthynnus alletteratus*.

Anglers should learn to identify the two species; one makes

good eating, the other makes great Gulf Stream trolling baits. The striped bonito is good to eat, like most tunas, when grilled or smoked. However, the spotted bonito has strong-flavored, bloody flesh that's not high on an angler's list of table fare. But by any name these tiny tunas are some of the most fun to catch of all the saltwater species when hooked on light tackle.

For my purposes in describing fishing techniques, I'll simply lump them together and call them both "bonito." Although this may not be entirely correct scientifically speaking, both of these fish put on similar battles and exhibit such a spectacle of speed and power that the fight mimics in miniature the famed fighting abilities of their huge cousins—the giant bluefin, bigeye and yellowfin tunas.

The presence of bonito within sight of land is news that spreads like a wildfire through the ranks of offshore anglers. Arriving just after bluefish make their appearance, the April run of bonito is anticipated as a rite of spring. The October run isn't as newsworthy because so many other desirable species are abundant in the fall, but bonitos do arrive in great numbers. Because neither striped nor spotted bonito are targeted by commercial fishermen they're always abundant during the right time of year. The only problem is that bad weather can prevent fishermen from heading out to catch them. The main competition for these fish is among recreational anglers, with boats often cutting off one another when trying to jump-fish small schools that surface just long enough for a cast or two and disappear as quickly as they appear.

The striped bonito tend to show up a little earlier than the spotted bonito because of temperature preference. Striped bonito like a temperature of 55 to 60 degrees, while spotted bonito prefer temperatures that range from 57 to 65 degrees. Both species can therefore be found at the same time and place, and are also often found mixing with schools of Spanish mackerel, which move in as the bonito action tapers off with warming temperatures in May, or as water temperature descends from the upper 60s in September.

Both bonito species achieve weights of 5 to 15 pounds. Their bodies are genetically adapted for high speed. Shaped like footballs, or according to scientific descriptions, having the ideal "fusiform" shape like the fuselage of a plane, these fish swim faster than any other small game fish. Their pectoral fins even tuck into folds in the sides of their bodies that are perfectly molded to the fins' contours thereby creating turbulence while the fish is swimming. At first glance the tiny tails that power their runs simply don't look like enough of a propeller to get the job done. But a bonito's entire body undulates to build up speeds that make lines sing as it cuts a wake across the surface of the ocean.

Fly-fishermen are especially fond of catching bonito because they readily take a hook and they're easy to cast to when they're visible because they're not timid. Many saltwater fly-fishing guides from all along the state's coastal regions head offshore from October through December during the spotted bonito runs. Catching a "Fat Albert" on a fly is a feat all saltwater fly-fisherman should experience in person to appreciate.

On the southern coast near Wrightsville Beach, the runs of striped bonito are legendary. Local fly-fishing guides take anglers out for these Atlantic bonito in March and April. Flies and poppers attract bonito on fly tackle and are sight-cast to surfacing fish.

Anglers can also troll lures along the edges of bonito schools to catch the fish. Sometimes the fish run deep, especially in the middle of the day. Planers used ahead of spoons or deep-diving lures draw strikes from bonito if the lures are trolled at the depth at which the fish are seen on a depthfinder screen. When the fish are on top, they're easy to catch while trolling *Clarkspoons*. When the fish are just beneath the surface, adding a trolling weight ahead of the lure will take it down to the fish. It's always important to use a wire, monofilament or fluorocarbon leader for catching striped bonito because their sharp teeth can clip lightweight monofilament lines.

Jump-fishing surfacing schools of bonito with spinning or baitcasting gear is probably the way most anglers catch the fish. Boats are maneuvered to the upwind side or at a perpendicular

147

An Atlantic bonito or "striped bonito" caught with a tinsel jig.

angle to the wind near an area where fish are seen surfacing. Casting into the wind presents distance problems since the lure will be held back and the boat will drift away from the fish school.

A floating popping plug, casting spoon, or bucktail jig is cast into the school and retrieved rapidly. The strike is fast and the subsequent run is furious. The fish are so aggressive that if one pulls free of the hooks, another fish usually strikes the lure before it can be retrieved all the way back to the boat.

With bonito, the type of lure is not as important as the lure presentation and its size. Bonito like their food on the run. Fast retrieves typically draw the most strikes. They feed on several types of minnows. If a few casts into a bonito school don't result in hook-ups, anglers should try observing the size of the baitfish that the fish are chasing and match the size of the lure to the bait. If a fish has been caught, it pays to check the stomach contents for the size of the forage species it's been eating.

Fishermen accustomed to catching other saltwater schooling species like bluefish, Spanish mackerel and king mackerel are simply not prepared to deal with the speed and endurance of large bonito. While most of the other game fish have blazing initial runs that strip line from fishing reels, bonito will often make several such runs. Subsequent runs make the drag scream as loudly as the first, and the fish usually ends up spiraling beneath the boat for long minutes before it's tired enough to be swung over the gunwale. This spiraling habit can twist lines badly unless a swivel is used ahead of the lure.

Landing bonito should not be accomplished with gaffs. When struck, the fish bleed badly and also spew forth stomach contents, which can make a boat deck very slippery and messy. Fish should be landed by grabbing the leader and swinging the fish directly into a fish box or by using a landing net with hard rubber mesh that won't foul hooks or be snagged by teeth.

Finding the action is easy. Bonito feed on smaller fish like anchovies, silversides and glass minnows. Seabirds prefer the same diet. When bonito drive the baitfish to the surface, skimmers, pelicans and gulls start dive-bombing them from the air. From their high vantage point, flying birds can spot action from miles away. All fishermen have to do is find the birds "working" the baitfish, and they'll have found the place to fish.

A pair of binoculars can be a big help when sight-fishing bonito schools. Not only does the magnification help fishermen to see the birds, it also helps in determining whether the fish are actually surfacing. Birds can see to great depths beneath the water surface. Sometimes they'll follow a school for miles before the fish come to the surface and will dip and dive without breaking into the water. Knowing for certain that the fish are on top and are easy targets before rushing across several miles of ocean makes an angler's fishing time more productive.

On days when the birds don't show, or in the middle of the day when the birds are full from the morning's feeding frenzy, an angler can look for other boats that are in on the action. Another tactic is to look for birds resting on the water's surface. Gulls like to sit on the water in areas where they know baitfish are present, waiting for bonito to drive them to the top. At times the feeding fish also leave an oil slick on the surface that can clue anglers to the presence of a bonito school because they can smell the slick's scent from several hundred yards downwind.

Chapter 22

Tussling With Tautogs

The weather had been as cold as it ever gets on the coast of North Carolina. Winter had set in as solid as the ice covering the puddles left behind by rainsqualls that had passed through three days earlier.

Of course, even in winter the air doesn't stay cold for long on the coast. The cold front passed, leaving in its wake balmy days with the mercury rising to 70 degrees.

A light wind rippled the inlet as we headed out in a 22-foot boat equipped with a cuddy cabin. The full-length windshield kept the dawn chill from making our eyes water as Jeff Stokley pointed the bow toward an artificial reef that was placed near a rock outcrop located 5 miles offshore.

An ice chest full of weakfish was the target of the trip. If the water had turned too cold for weakfish, perhaps a few Virginia mullet would take their place in the cooler.

It shouldn't have been a surprise that the temperature gauge on the dash gave a Fahrenheit reading of 45 degrees at the water surface. The big surprise was that large fish showed up on the depthfinder screen. They were suspended just off the bottom and appeared to be weakfish. However, jigging spoons in their faces brought no response at all.

"'Togs, I'll bet," I said to Stokley. "When the water gets this cold, they're the only big fish around that stay this close to shore."

Stokley's forehead wrinkled as he fine-tuned a knob on the sonar machine.

"What in the world is a 'tog?" Stokley asked.

Fortunately, we had brought aboard some fresh shrimp to use

Jeff Stokley caught this fat tautog on a piece of shrimp dropped to the bottom at an artificial reef.

as weakfish and Virginia mullet bait. Quickly rigging two No. 4 long-shank hooks on a double-hook bottom rig and tying the rig to a spinning outfit, I prepared to cast it over the side.

Stokley circled the area and located the highest concentration of fish on the bottom, then switched off the motor. We cast our baits and allowed them to drift along, barely tickling the bottom. After a drift of a few yards, Stokley's rod bent double with the first strike.

"Wow! This guy can pull!" he grunted.

The drag washers slipped and the reel's clicker screeched as the fish dug for the bottom in its struggle to escape. Once the fish locked the line around something hard on the rocky bottom. But the leader held and the fish was eventually pumped to the surface.

"What in the world is that?" Stokley asked while I scooped the fish from the water with a landing net.

"That, my friend, is a Yankee fish," I said. "Tautogs are cold-water fish and are a preferred bottom fish up North. But most anglers along the North Carolina coast don't even know what one is and even toss them overboard if they catch one."

"It sure looks too ugly to eat." Stokley said.

Tossing the fish into the ice chest, I smiled at the thought of the good eating we would have when we got back home that afternoon. Circling the area, we stayed on top of the school of 'togs and caught half a dozen that weighed from 2 to 5 pounds each. That's not a bad day of fishing when there's nothing else to catch without heading a far distance offshore to find warmer water. The fillets of a tautog are as white as the flesh of a grouper. In spite of their strange appearance—an overstuffed fish with mottled brown skin and large lips covering jutting incisors—tautogs are fine-eating fish as well as absolute brutes to catch when hooked on light tackle. A 20-pound 'tog is not at all rare, and winning the fight with a big one can make an angler feel like he's earned his dinner.

The tautog is a fish that anglers can catch when the winter doldrums have set in. However, its habits are unknown to many offshore anglers along the North Carolina coast.

Tautogs feed on shellfish. They have forward-projecting teeth that are extremely sturdy pegs and are perfect for crushing hard shells. The inside of their mouths are also hard. When fishing for very large tautogs, anglers who know what they're doing choose large, sturdy hooks of size No. 2 and up that can reach inside the mouth to penetrate the palate of the fish. However, for fish below 5 pounds in weight that are more typical for southern waters, anglers can use small hooks and take advantage of the thick outer lips that cover the teeth of a tautog. A tautog typically tastes his food by nipping at it with his teeth before swallowing. At the first sensation of a fish taking the bait, an angler should set the hook. A solid hook-up in the lip when using a light-action spinning rod will keep enough pressure off the hook to prevent it from tearing free and nearly always bring the fish to the boat.

Tautogs are found around hard structure that holds lots of mollusks and crustaceans. Jetties, rock outcrops, wrecks, coral reefs and artificial reefs are all likely to hold tautogs when the water is so cold that nothing else is biting.

Anglers who target tautogs should shun using fish for bait, and that's why many anglers are unfamiliar with them. Clams, crabs and shrimp are the best baits to use. Freezing these baits when they're easy to collect during the warmer months can be the ticket to tussling with tautogs when cold weather sets in. Whether frozen or not, baits should be as fresh as possible to attract the most attention from tautogs.

It can be difficult to think that far ahead but that's what it takes to tussle with a tautog. When winter's chill is in the air, smart anglers will be glad they remembered to collect their baits during the summer months. Heading out to catch a few fat tautogs for the frying pan will warm their hearts, while anglers who never heard of the fish are merely wishing they were fishing and staying home.

Epilogue

This is the age of information and successful offshore angling depends upon not only having good information, but the best information. Having read this far, the fisherman should have found *Offshore Angler* to be one of the best saltwater fishing resources ever published.

A successful trip outside any inlet depends upon an immense amount of preparation and forethought as to boat selection, rigging, weather, safety gear, tackle and, finally, what fish may be biting and where they might be found. This also adds up to a great amount of cost in terms of money and time. Fuel consumption, boat and motor wear, missed work hours, and buying baits, rigs and lures all adds up to great monetary cost. Hopefully, *Offshore Angler* will have helped the mackerel boat fisherman save time by providing the knowledge it takes to catch fish that could otherwise only be earned by spending many years on the water. Knowledge saves time and saving time conserves money.

It takes that hard-to-come-by combination of knowledge, time and money to spend even the briefest time fishing in the ocean. But, in spite of the effort involved, offshore angling sure is fun!

Offshore Angler was not written with the expectation that it will remain in a house. By the time an angler heads out to sea, its pages should be well worn from thumbs searching for favorite chapters, as well as discolored by motor oil, spilled coffee and reel lube. Saltwater, chum and bait drippings should begin to perfume its pages as it's carried to tackle shops for help in questioning the experts manning the bait counters, then placed on the steering console of a mackerel boat. Through use, its wisdom should become part of the thinking process that makes an *Offshore Angler* increasingly successful at an avocation commonly referred to as a "second job." Anyone who doesn't believe that statement has only to look at a few boat names to see that a reference to the captain's way of earning a living is a common theme.

Buying a copy of *Offshore Angler* costs about as much as a trolling lure or a box of saltwater hooks. Yet there are many fishermen who, unfortunately for them, will not pick it up to flip through the pages. Unlike a computer, it's easy to take along for a quick reference at sea. The Artificial Reef Guide and photos are nearly as helpful as having an experienced mate onboard. Catch a big fish? Look it up in the glossary to see if it's a contender for world record status or if it should be eaten or released.

This book was made possible by experienced anglers who shared their knowledge. As new fishermen hone their skills, they should in turn pass them on to others with less experience.

While the expert advice held within these pages is guaranteed to make anyone a better fisherman, that knowledge must be held in the highest moral regard. All size and bag limits for game fish must be strictly followed and any fish that's not intended for immediate use should be returned, unharmed, to the water. Every animal has a purpose. Even non-target fish commonly regarded as nuisances by anglers have their places in the natural order and must be appreciated as part of the cycle of life in the sea.

It must always be remembered that while catching fish can enhance the enjoyment of a day on the water, it should never become the ultimate goal. All offshore anglers should enjoy seeing the splendor of a sunrise exploding through a cloud as the boat crests an inlet's final wave. The rich aroma of fish, the salty scent of sea spray and the fumes of outboard motor exhaust wafting on the wind should fill their nostrils with memories that help them get through mundane days when they're waiting for winds to calm or workweeks to end. Successful fishermen revel as much in hearing a scolding flock of gulls or showering school of baitfish as in the scream of a reel at the instant of a strike and a fellow angler's shouts of "Fish On!"

North Carolina
Artificial Reef Guide

Using the
Artificial Reef Guide

The data presented in the Artificial Reef Guide is designed for use by fishermen. It is not intended for use as an aid to navigation.

For the most efficient use of the data in finding and catching fish, anglers should utilize the best electronic navigation and sonar equipment they can afford. They should use caution when anchoring near any artificial reef because anchors can become irretrievably hung. Anglers who fish artificial reefs should educate themselves on the various anchor styles and anchoring methods recommended for use around hard structure.

Artificial reefs undergo a detailed permitting process and are maintained by the North Carolina Division of Marine Fisheries (NCDMF). Many types of structure have been deployed at artificial reefs including used tires, barges, ships, railroad boxcars, concrete rubble, concrete pipe and Reef Balls.

Concrete is becoming the preferred material because it presents the fewest environmental problems. Tires have floated away from reefs. Ships require extensive cleaning before they can be deployed. Metal boxcars deteriorate in saltwater.

Deterioration has made material at some artificial reefs difficult to locate. NCDMF has therefore undertaken an extensive program to locate as much of the existing material as possible and provide accurate coordinates to fishermen.

The coordinates in this Artificial Reef Guide are the most accurate ever published. However, they still have varying degrees of accuracy. The accompanying maps were originally published by NCDMF in *North Carolina Reef Guide* and are only provided to give anglers a visual representation of the general orientation of some of the originally deployed reef material. Anglers should refer to the coordinates for accurate locations of structure because much has been added since the maps were originally assembled. Marker buoys may also shift or be temporarily dislodged by storms.

Jim Francesconi is the NCDMF Artificial Reef Coordinator and works out of the Division's office in Morehead City. Francesconi provided fishermen with some of his valuable insight about using the data for finding structure at artificial reefs. He also explained why some pieces of structure are located more accurately than others.

"The earliest deployments of material utilized Loran coordinates," Francesconi said. "We did not make any Loran to GPS conversions. These locations have variable degrees of accuracy.

"Some of the sites were located by side-scan radar and some by soundings. Some locations were made by side-scan sonar in conjunction with GPS. These locations are fairly accurate.

"On sites where we use only deployment data with a GPS reading taken at the surface the data can be off by 75 feet. This applies mostly to pipe deployed since 2000.

"Some material was located based on existing data by using a fishfinder. Divers then made underwater verification of the structure and a sent pop-up float to the surface where a GPS reading were taken on the float. Some locations were made with a fishfinder and the location of the material was obvious. These locations have the highest degree of accuracy.

"Sea state can make an artificial reef difficult to find. For example, Reef Balls can look like waves on a fishfinder screen. Anglers should watch their fishfinder for bait. If bait is off the bottom, it is usually down current of the material. Anglers should also watch for large individual marks on the bottom. These will be the bottom-dwelling species that are usually right on top of the reef.

"If anglers can't locate an artificial reef, they should use a square search pattern beginning at the coordinates. They should go north a couple of marks, then one side, then back south beyond the starting point and around again. Expanding the search area in a methodical fashion will help them locate the structure."

159

In the Artificial Reef Guide, reef structure locations marked with an asterisk (*) have the highest degree of accuracy. This structure was located by divers or by obvious sonar verification with GPS coordinates taken at the site. Artificial Reefs are listed in numerical order.

For further information on artificial reef deployments and updated coordinates, or recreational fishing size and bag limits, anglers should contact NCDMF at (800) 682-2632,
(252) 726-7021
or visit the website at www.ncdmf.net.

NORTH CAROLINA ARTIFICIAL REEFS

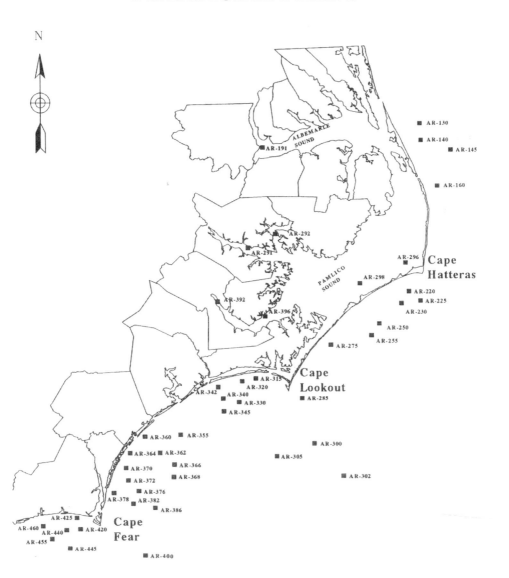

N

AR-130
AR-140
AR-145

AR-160

ALBEMARLE SOUND
AR-191

AR-292
AR-291

AR-296
Cape
Hatteras

PAMLICO
SOUND
AR-298
AR-220
AR-225
AR-230

AR-392
AR-396

AR-250
AR-255

AR-275

Cape
Lookout

AR-315
AR-320
AR-342
AR-340
AR-330
AR-285
AR-345

AR-360
AR-355
AR-300
AR-364
AR-362
AR-305
AR-370
AR-366
AR-372
AR-368
AR-302
AR-376
AR-378
AR-382
AR-386

AR-425
Cape
Fear
AR-460
AR-440
AR-420
AR-455
AR-445
AR-400

AR #130

Average Depth 55-60 feet

		GPS	LORAN
	Buoy	*36° 00.192' / 075° 31.800'	26979.1 / 40726.0

Deployment Date	Reef Material	GPS	LORAN
23 Nov-86 12 Dec-86	Box Cars: 10	(200 - 500' SW of Buoy)	
28-Nov.-00	Reef Balls: 300	36° 00.183' / 075° 31.833'	
		36° 00.183' / 075° 31.800'	
		36° 00.183' / 075° 31.883'	
		36° 00.133' / 075° 31.817' .	
	Bridge Pile Cutoff	36° 00.217' / 075° 31.867'	

AR #140

Range 001° magnetic — 8.9nm from Oregon Inlet Sea

Average Depth 57 feet

		GPS	LORAN
	Buoy	*35° 56.741' / 075° 31.781'	26975.0 / 40690.0

Deployment Date	Reef Material	GPS	LORAN
23-Nov-86	Box Cars: 10	(200 - 500' SW to NW of Buoy)	26975.0/40690.5
			26975.0/40690.0
13-Jun-89	130' barge	*35° 56.683' / 075° 31.917'	26975.1/40689.1
15-Jun-89	130' barge	*35° 56.750' / 075° 31.917'	26975.0/40690.0
14-Nov-98	Pipe	36° 56.767' / 075° 23.750'	
23-Nov-98	Pipe	36° 56.917' / 075° 31.767'	

map continued on next page...

AR #140

N

Boxcars

Barge

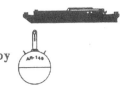

Buoy

Barge

Yards

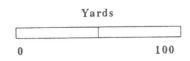

0   100

AR #145
LCU-145

Range 049° magnetic — 8.1nm from Oregon Inlet Sea Buoy

Average Depth 65 feet

		GPS	LORAN
	Buoy	*35° 54.017' / 075° 23.883'	26941.4 / 40685.7

Deployment Date	Reef Material	GPS	LORAN
12-Jan-87	115' landing craft (LCU)	*35° 54.067' / 075° 23.933'	26941.4 / 40685.5 to 40685.6
1991	4 areas - bridge rubble	*35° 53.967' / 075° 23.933'	26941.9 / 40684.7
		35° 53.883' / 075° 23.950'	26941.9 / 40684.3
		35° 53.950' / 075° 23.983'	26941.8 / 40684.2
		36° 00.133' / 075° 31.817'	26941.6 / 40684.5
			26941.4 / 40684.7
			26941.5 / 40684.0
1994	185' vessel "Advance II"	*35° 54.000' / 075° 23.867'	26941.2 / 40685.3
			26941.5 / 40685.0
	Small Load of Pipe	35° 54.100' / 075° 23.867' to 35° 54.067' / 075° 23.817'	
	Lg. Load of Pipe	35° 53.983' / 075° 23.967'	

map continued on next page...

AR #145

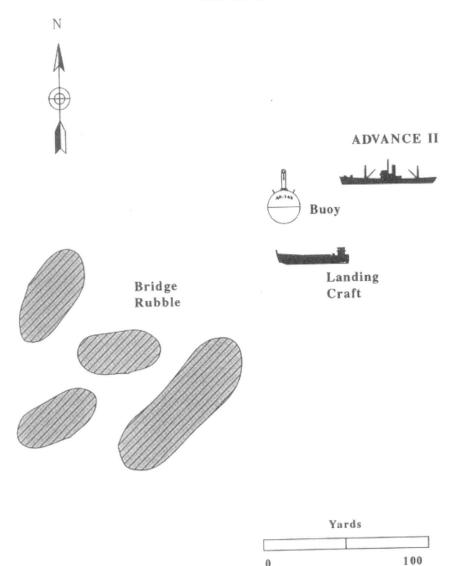

N

ADVANCE II

Buoy

Bridge
Rubble

Landing
Craft

Yards

0   100

AR #160
Oregon Inlet Reef

Range 150° magnetic — 4.4nm from Oregon Inlet Sea Buoy

Average Depth 66 feet

		GPS	LORAN
	Buoy	*35° 43.888' / 075° 26.771'	26940.7 / 40574.1

Deployment Date	Reef Material	GPS	LORAN
12-Dec-74	440' ship "Zane Gray"	*35° 43.817' / 075° 26.767'	26940.7 / 40574.1
	83' trawler "Irving H"		26940.3 / 40575.1 (old numbers, site needs inspection to locate)
30-Nov-78	440' ship "Dionysus"	*35° 44.033' / 075° 26.733'	26940.9 / 40576.3
30-Nov-78	Part of the "Dionysus"	*35° 44.000' / 075° 26.733'	26940.8 / 40576.8
	8 units concrete VanDoren	35° 43.900' / 075° 26.867'	
		35° 43.933' / 075° 26.867'	27242.9 / 39078.9 to 27242.8 / 39078.1
8-Dec-99	Piling pieces	35° 43.933' / 075° 26.900'	26941.4 / 40574.6 (250 yds. WNW of buoy)
8-Dec-99	Reef Balls	35° 43.883' / 075° 26.833'	26941.0 / 40574.9 (150 - 200 yds. WNW of buoy)
15-Aug-00	Reef Balls	35° 43.867' / 075° 26.817'	
15-Aug-00	115 Pilings	35° 43.917' / 075° 26.883'	

map continued on next page...

AR #160

N

DIONYSUS

ZANE GRAY

Buoy

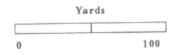

Yards

0   100

AR #220

Range 111° magnetic — 4.9nm from Hatteras Inlet Sea Buoy

Average Depth 64 feet

		GPS	LORAN
		*35° 08.117' / 077° 40.633'	26951.0 / 40182.0

Deployment Date	Reef Material	GPS	LORAN
12-Dec-86	Box cars: 9		26951.3 / 40181.3
			26951.3 / 40181.0
			26951.0 / 40181.4
			26951.8 / 40181.3
			26951.7 / 40181.5
			26951.7 / 40181.3
			26951.6 / 40181.3
15-Dec-86	5 pieces concrete (75 tons)		(100-600' SW of buoy)
1993	Concrete pieces	*35° 08.067' / 075° 40.633'	26951.3 / 40181.7 to 26951.2 / 40181.3
	Reef Balls: 200 (2 Tracks)	35° 08.133' / 075° 40.500'	NE
		35° 08.050' / 075° 40.500'	SE
		35° 08.050' / 075° 40.617'	SW
	Reef Balls: 200 (2 Tracks cont)	35° 08.117' / 075° 40.567'	NW

AR #225

Range 120° magnetic — 6.2nm from Hatteras Inlet Sea Buoy

Average Depth 69 feet

		GPS	LORAN
Buoy		*35° 06.750' / 075° 39.233'	26945.0 / 40175.0

Deployment Date	Reef Material	GPS	LORAN
12-Dec-86	Box cars: 8		26945.9 / 40175.7
	Concrete pieces: 7 (105 tons)		26945.6 / 40175.3
			to
			26945.2 / 40173.0
			26945.5 / 40175.3
			(200-600' SW of buoy)

Additional Comments:

Inspection found a rock ledge at 26945.2 / 40173.0. This ledge is 1-2 feet in height and runs about NE-SW for about 250 yards.

AR #230
Mr. J.C. Reef

Range 120° magnetic — 6.2nm from Hatteras Inlet Sea Buoy

Average Depth 72 feet

		GPS	LORAN
Buoy		35° 06.133' / 075° 42.933'	26957.0 / 40155.0

Deployment Date	Reef Material	GPS	LORAN
15-Sep-87	105' tug "Mr. J.C."	*35° 06.117' / 075° 42.967'	26957.0 / 40155.0
			26957.3 / 40154.9
13-Jun-05	130' yard freighter	*35° 06.183' / 075° 42.967'	26957.3 / 40155.1
			to
			26957.3 / 40155.3
1991	75' landing craft		26957.4 / 40155.6

map continued on next page...

AR #230

N

 Landing
Craft

 Yard
Freighter

Tug MR. J.C.   Buoy

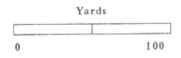

Yards

0   100

AR #250

Range 156° magnetic — 5.1nm from Ocracoke Inlet Sea Buoy

Average Depth 83 feet

		GPS	LORAN
	Buoy	*34° 56.900' / 075° 54.867'	26987.3 / 40024.0

Deployment Date	Reef Material	GPS	LORAN
14-Nov-86	Box cars: 10		26986.9 / 40023.5
			(200 - 600' SW of buoy)
1990 - 1992	Concrete rubble	*34° 56.917' / 075° 54.767'	26987.2 / 40024.2
		*34° 56.967' / 075° 54.783'	26987.3 / 40024.3
		*34° 56.917' / 075° 54.817'	26987.0 / 40023.6
		*34° 56.967' / 075° 54.850'	26987.4 / 40023.6
		*34° 56.933' / 075° 54.833	26987.3 / 40024.1
		*34° 56.983' / 075° 54.833'	
		*34° 56.983' / 075° 54.817'	
3-May-01	220' steel bridge span, old Fairfield Bridge	34° 56.983' / 075° 54.817'	
		34° 56.800' / 075° 54.800'	

map continued on next page...

173

AR #250

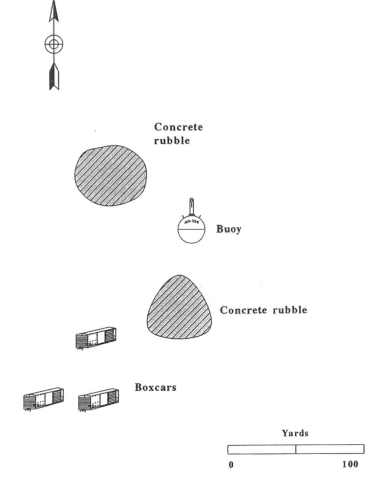

N

Concrete
rubble

Buoy

Concrete rubble

Boxcars

Yards

0   100

174

AR #255

Range 184° magnetic — 6.1nm from Ocracoke Inlet Sea Buoy

		GPS	LORAN
	Buoy	*34° 55.483' / 075° 57.917'	26995.9 / 39998.0

Average Depth 84 feet

Deployment Date	Reef Material	GPS	LORAN
14 Nov-86	Box cars: 10	*34° 55.533' / 075° 57.867'	26995.7 / 39997.9
15 Dec-86			(100-500' SW of buoy)
		34° 55.467' / 075° 57.950'	26995.7 / 39998.0
			26995.9 / 39998.1
			26995.8 / 39997.7
	150' steel bridge span, old Hobucken Bridge	*34° 55.517' / 075° 57.867'	
		34° 55.467' / 075° 57.95'	
	Pipe	*34° 55.483' / 075° 57.983'	
	High profile units	* 34° 55.500' / 075° 57.900'	
	Concrete rubble	* 34° 55.533' / 075° 57.950'	
		to	
		* 34°55.517 / 075°57.867	26995.9 / 39998.5

map continued on next page...

AR #255

Yards

0   100

Concrete rubble

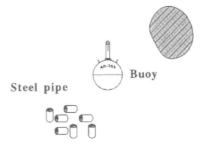

Buoy

Steel pipe

Boxcars

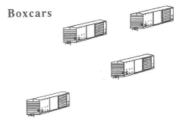

176

AR #275
Drum Inlet

Range 140° magnetic — 2.0nm from North end of Drum Inlet
Average Depth 55 feet

		GPS	LORAN
	Buoy	*34° 50.100' / 075° 16.983'	27052.0 / 39870.2

Deployment Date	Reef Material	GPS	LORAN
1991 1993	Concrete pipes (Includes 700 pieces 4' x 8' and 40 pieces of large concrete pipe)	*34° 50.067' / 076° 17.017' to 34° 50.033' / 076°17.017'	27051.9 / 39870.3
		34° 50.100' / 075° 16.983'	27051.7 / 39870.1 to 27051.7 / 39870.2
			27051.6 / 39870.4 to 27051.6 / 39870.5
			27051.7 / 39869.6
			27052.0 / 39870.0
			27051.9 / 39869.7 to 27051.9 / 39869.3
			27052.0 / 39869.4
			27051.9 / 39869.1
			27051.9 / 39868.9
			27051.9 / 39869.0
			27051.9 / 39870.1
			27051.8 / 39869.1
1992	65' crew boat "Miss Clara"	*34° 50.150' / 076° 16.850'	27051.7 / 39870.9
	130' ship "Gulf Coast"	*34° 50.117' / 076° 16.617'	
29-Feb-00	Reef Balls	34° 50.133' / 076° 17.000' to 34°50.117' / 076° 17.017'	27052.2 / 39870.3 to 27052.2 / 39870.1

177

map continued on next page...

AR #275

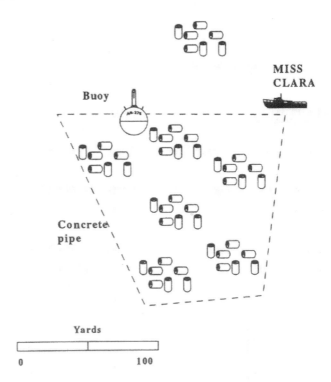

N

MISS CLARA

Buoy

Concrete pipe

Yards

0   100

178

AR #285

George Summerlin Reef

Range 125° magnetic — 3.5nm from East Cape Lookout Shoals Slough buoy (RW "E")

Average Depth 65 feet

		GPS	LORAN
	Buoy	*34° 33.383' / 076° 26.350'	27062.2 / 39682.7

Deployment Date	Reef Material	GPS	LORAN
31-Jan-89	130' steel hull fishing vessel "NANCY LEE"	*34° 33.533' / 076° 26.200' to 34° 33.367' / 076° 26.200'	27062.2 / 39683.3
1991	Concrete pipes	*34° 33.567' / 076° 26.250'	27062.2 / 39683.1
1993	Concrete pipes	*34° 33.467' / 076° 26.300'	27062.6 / 39682.7
		*34° 33.500' / 076° 26.283'	27062.3 / 39682.0
		34° 33.367' / 076° 26.200'	
			27062.3 / 39681.8 and 27062.3 / 39682.3
	High Profile Units	*34° 33.350' / 076° 26.333'	
6-Mar-00	Reef Balls	34° 33.383' / 076° 26.383' to 34° 33.350' / 076° 26.400'	27062.5 / 39680.8 to 27062.6 / 39680.5

Additional Comments:

Includes 500 pieces of 5' x 8' concrete pipe and 50 pieces of large concrete pipe.

map continued on next page...

AR #285

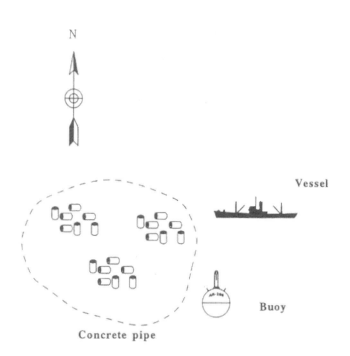

N

Vessel

Concrete pipe

Buoy

Yards

0   100

180

AR #300
Hardees Reef

Range 153° magnetic — 24.0nm from Beaufort Inlet sea buoy		
Average Depth 90 feet		
	GPS	**LORAN**
No Buoy on this site	Reef located 500 yards N of 14 buoy (R "14")	

Deployment Date	Reef Material	GPS	LORAN
29-Jan-89	174 ft yard oiler FS-26	*34° 18.517' / 076° 24.133'	27039.3 / 39574.3 27039.1 / 39575.1
1991	Concrete pipes	*34° 18.517' / 076° 24.300'	27039.4 / 39575.0 (center of pipe)
		*34° 18.633' / 076° 24.150'	27039.2 / 39575.0 (Includes 1000 pieces 4' x 8' concrete pipe)
1993	Concrete pipes	*34° 18.633' / 076° 24.183'	27039.4 / 39574.8* (Includes 500 pieces 4' x 8' concrete pipe)
		*34° 18.617' / 076° 24.133'	27039.4 / 39575.1 27039.5 / 39573.4 27039.2 / 39575.2
		*34° 18.567' / 076° 24.533'	
		*34° 18.467' / 076° 24.567'	
		*34° 18.533' / 076° 24.550'	
		*34° 18.417' / 076° 24.600	
		*34° 18.600' / 076° 24.550' to 34° 18.167' / 076° 24.550'	

map continued on next page...

AR #300

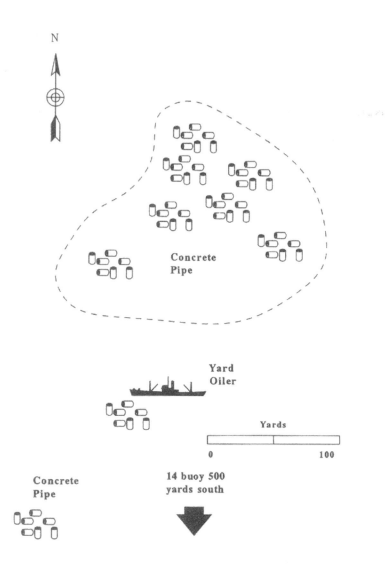

N

Concrete
Pipe

Yard
Oiler

Yards

0   100

Concrete
Pipe

14 buoy 500
yards south

AR #302
Yancey

Range 143° magnetic — 35.4nm from Beaufort Inlet sea buoy

Average Depth 160 feet

		GPS	LORAN
	No Buoy on this site		

Deployment Date	Reef Material	GPS	LORAN
Mar / Apr-89	425 FADS		27001.0 / 39566.1 (center of mass)
12-Jun-90	459 ft assault transport "YANCEY"	34° 10.233' / 076° 13.750' (South end)	26998.8 / 39567.3
			26998.7 / 39568.0 (North end)
13-Jun-91	Concrete Pipe	34° 10.267' / 076° 13.767' to 34° 10.283' / 076° 13.783'	26999.1 / 39567.7
		34° 10.283' / 076° 13.800'	26999.0 / 39567.5
15-Jun-93	Concrete Pipe	34° 10.267' / 076° 13.750' to 34° 10.233' / 076° 13.733'	26998.6 / 39567.9
		34° 10.200' / 076° 13.733'	26998.7 / 39567.3
			26998.8 / 39567.1
			26999.1 / 39566.8

Additional Comments:

FADS sunk in a 0.5 mile circle around center point, 80-100' below surface, reduced to bottom material.

AR #305
Carteret County Sportfishing Association Reef

Range 184° magnetic — 22.5nm from Beaufort Inlet sea buoy

Average Depth 104 feet

		GPS	LORAN
	No Buoy on this site		

Deployment Date	Reef Material	GPS	LORAN
29-Jul-88	439 ft ex-USN	*34° 16.683' / 076° 38.650'	27081.4 / 39489.7
	cable layer "AEOLUS"	(Originally sunk at 27081.4 / 39489.7)	
		*34° 16.700' / 076° 38.633'	

AR #315
Atlantic Beach Reef

Range 300° magnetic — 3.9nm from Beaufort Inlet sea buoy

Average Depth 49 feet

		GPS	LORAN
	Buoy	*34° 40.333' / 076° 44.667'	27128.0 / 39660.8

Deployment Date	Reef Material	GPS	LORAN
4-Jun-74	440' liberty ship "THEODORE PARKER"	* 34° 40.350' / 076° 44.717' to	
		34° 40.350' / 076° 44.767'	27128.0 / 39660.8
			27128.0 / 39660.9
			27127.3 / 39662.5
1980	40' Coast Guard launch	27127.8 / 39659.5	
6-Jan-83	Trawler "HELEN MAY"		
2002	Newport DOT Concrete Pipe	34° 40.316' / 076° 44.804' (West of Tug TAKOS)	
2003	Newport DOT Concrete Pipe, Misc. Concrete, Assorted Can Units, Radio Island Pilings	34° 40.330' / 076° 44.793' (East of Tug TAKOS)	
	Radio Island Ramp Pilings (6-12' length, ~500 pieces)	34° 40.280' / 076° 44.534' (NE end)	
	Radio Island Ramp Pilings (6-12' length, ~500 pieces)	34° 40.217' / 076° 44.617' (SW end)	
	(Heavy Concentration)	34° 40.243' / 076° 44.600'	
2-Nov-00	104' Navy tug "TAKOS"	34° 40.333' / 076° 44.783'	27128.1 / 39661.4

continued

185

Deployment Date	Material	GPS	LORAN
1992	Aircraft A-4 (2)	34° 40.367' / 076° 44.650'	27127.9 / 39661.5
			27127.8 / 39661.4
1991, 1992	Concrete rubble	*34° 40.383' / 076° 44.650'	
		to	
		34° 40.383' / 076° 44.667'	27127.7 / 39660.6
			and
			27128.07 / 39661.6
	Bridge Rubble	34° 39.967' / 076° 45.050'	
		to	
		34° 39.983' / 076° 45.033'	
1989	Steel bridge framing	34° 40.350' / 076° 44.583'	27127.7 / 39661.9
21-Feb-00	Reef Balls	34° 40.383' / 076° 44.500'	
		to	
		34° 40.400' / 076° 44.517'	27127.4 / 39662.4
		34° 40.400' / 076° 44.500'	
		34° 40.400' / 076° 44.483'	
2003	Pilings (Round Disperse Pattern)	34° 39.908' / 076° 45.189' (West of Broadcast Dump)	
	Broadcast Dump (Quadrat Area Coord.)	34° 39.957 / 076° 45.129' NW	
		34° 39.925' / 076° 45.062' NE	
		34° 39.863' / 076° 45.085' SE	
		34° 39.839' / 076° 45.156' SW	

Additional Comments:

177,168 tires were added to the site between 1974 and 1984.

map continued on next page...

AR #315

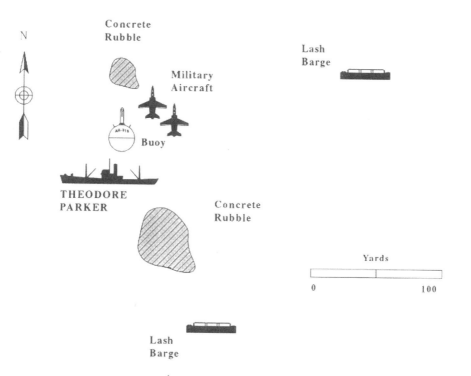

AR #320
Clinton Moss Reef

Range 282° magnetic — 6.4nm from Beaufort Inlet sea buoy

Average Depth 50 feet

		GPS	LORAN
Buoy		*34° 39.533' / 076° 48.417'	27138.6 / 39637.3

Deployment Date	Reef Material	GPS	LORAN
9-Jul-86	140' menhaden vessel "NOVELTY"	*34° 39.483' / 076° 48.433'	27138.5 / 39636.9
26-May-87 to 31-Dec-87	Atlantic Beach bridge rubble, 2 rows running N-S starting 100' E and 300' W of the "NOVELTY"	*34° 39.483' / 076° 48.450'	27138.6 / 39636.3 to 27138.6 / 39636.7
		34° 39.400' / 076° 48.450'	27138.6 / 39636.9
		34° 39.517' / 076° 48.433' to 34° 39.517' / 076° 48.467'	27138.4 / 39635.7 to 27138.4 / 39635.8
1990	Concrete pre-fab	34° 39.517' / 076° 48.433'	27138.5 / 39637.0
	Atlantic Beach bridge steel truss span	34° 39.483' / 076° 48.450' to 34° 39.517' / 076° 48.467'	

map continued on next page...

AR #320

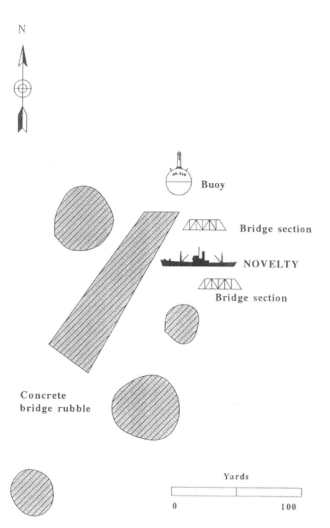

N

Buoy

Bridge section

NOVELTY

Bridge section

Concrete
bridge rubble

Yards

0   100

AR #330
Howard Chapin Reef

Range 247° magnetic — 10.0nm from Beaufort Inlet sea buoy

Average Depth 60 feet

		GPS	LORAN
Buoy		*34° 33.634 / 076° 51.267'	27139.7 / 39569.5

Deployment Date	Reef Material	GPS	LORAN
1986	Train Box Cars	*34° 33.633' / 076° 51.350' to	27139.6 / 39568.4 (200-500' SW of buoy)
		34° 33.633' / 076° 51.367'	
		*34° 33.550' / 076° 51.333'	27140.0 / 39568.8
		*34° 33.583' / 076° 51.367'	27140.2 / 39569.0
		*34° 33.550' / 076° 51.367'	27139.7 / 39569.0
		*34° 33.550' / 076° 51.317'	27139.7 / 39569.3
1992	320' landing craft repair ship "INDRA"	*34° 33.700' / 076° 51.100'	27139.5 / 39570.2
			27139.5 / 39570.8
1994	C-130 aircraft (2)	*34° 33.633' / 076° 51.367' to	
		34° 33.633' / 076° 51.383'	27140.0 / 39569.4
			27140.2 / 39568.9
1995	F-4 aircraft (1)	34° 33.633' / 076° 51.350' to	
		34° 33.633' / 076° 51.367'	27140.0 / 39569.3
	Can units (43)	*34° 33.700' / 076° 51.400'	
11-Sep-00	Can Units	34° 33.450' / 076° 51.450' to	
		34° 33.450' / 076° 51.483'	

AR #330 continued

Deployment Date	Reef Material	GPS	LORAN
1990	Fiberglass Pre-fabricated Domes	* 34° 33.783' / 076° 51.267'	
		*34° 33.767' / 076° 51.250'	
		*34° 33.733' / 076° 51.333'	
	Old concrete pipe: 41 pieces	*34° 33.617' / 076° 51.200'	
	New concrete pipes: 160 pieces	*34° 33.583' / 076° 51.200'	
11-Sep-00	Reef Balls: 45	34° 33.450' / 076° 51.383' to 34° 33.450' / 076° 51.417'	
	Concrete Pipe(600 tons)	34° 33.589' / 076° 51.438'	
	(Concentrations to SW)	34° 33.587' / 076° 51.445'	
		34° 33.580' / 076° 51.442	

map continued on next page...

191

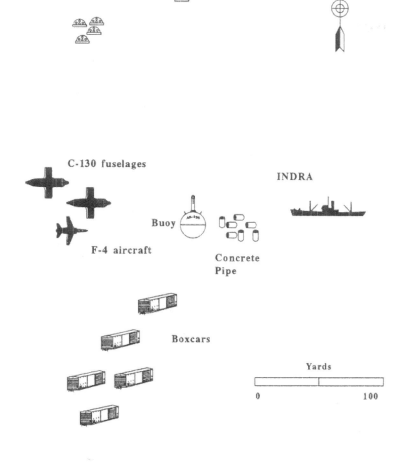

Domes

N

C-130 fuselages

INDRA

Buoy

F-4 aircraft

Concrete
Pipe

Boxcars

Yards

0   100

AR #340
J. Paul Tyndall Reef

Range 129° magnetic — 7.0nm from Bogue Inlet sea buoy

Average Depth 58 feet

		GPS	LORAN
	Buoy	*34° 34.350' / 076° 58.300'	27162.4 / 39545.3

Deployment Date	Reef Material	GPS	LORAN
29-Nov-86	Box cars: 10	*34° 34.317' / 076° 58.350' to	27162.2 / 39544.8 (200-500' SW of
		34° 34.300' / 076° 58.367'	Buoy)
		34° 34.283' / 076° 58.350'	27162.4 / 39544.7
			27162.6 / 39544.9
			27162.4 / 39544.4
			27162.3 / 39544.5
			27162.3 / 39544.4
1991	Concrete pipes: (1000) 500 are 5' x 8'	*34° 34.317' / 076° 58.350'	27162.3 / 39546.0
1993	500 pieces of concrete pipe	*34° 34.383' / 076° 58.300'	27162.2 / 39546.5
		*34° 34.367' / 076° 58.283'	27162.1 / 39545.8
		*34° 34.350' / 076° 58.250'	27162.4 / 39546.3
		*34° 34.317' / 076° 58.317'	27162.2 / 39545.6
		*34° 34.317' / 076° 58.300'	27162.6 / 39546.0
		*34° 34.333' / 076° 58.283'	27162.4 / 39545.7
		*34° 34.350' / 076° 58.267'	27162.5 / 39545.8
		*34° 34.350' / 076° 58.300'	27162.4 / 39545.3
		*34° 34.367' / 076° 58.317'	27162.3 / 39546.1
			27162.4 / 39546.0

continued

AR #340 continued

Deployment Date	Reef Material	GPS	LORAN
1993	Hatteras boat molds: 12	*34° 34.450' / 076° 58.500'	
		*34° 34.500' / 076° 58.517'	
		*34° 34.417' / 076° 58.483'	
		*34° 34.433' / 076° 58.517'	
		*34° 34.400' / 076° 58.483'	
		*34° 34.367' / 076° 58.533'	
		*34° 34.400' / 076° 58.533'	
		*34° 34.383' / 076° 58.517'	
		*34° 34.367' / 076° 58.500'	
		*34° 34.367' / 076° 58.333'	
		*34° 34.383' / 076° 58.500'	
3-Oct-00	Reef Balls: 25	34° 34.517' / 076° 58.433'	27162.9 / 39546.1
5-Oct-00	Reef Balls: 46	34° 34.533' / 076° 58.450'	
		34° 34.550' / 076° 58.433'	
		34° 34.517' / 076° 58.417'	
		34° 34.500' / 076° 58.450'	
		34° 34.517' / 076° 58.417'	
		34° 34.517' / 076° 58.433'	

map continued on next page...

AR #340

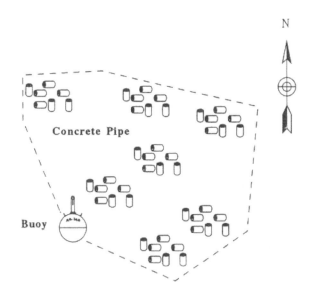

Concrete Pipe

Buoy

N

Boxcars

Yards

0   100

AR #342
Bogue Reef Inlet

Range 124° magnetic — 3.0nm from Bogue Inlet sea buoy

Average Depth 49 feet

		GPS	LORAN
	Buoy	*34° 36.533' / 077° 02.183'	27177.0 / 39549.8

Deployment Date	Reef Material	GPS	LORAN
20-May-86	Box cars: 10	34° 36.467' / 077° 02.167'	27177.1 / 39548.2 (1986 LORAN; 100-300' S and W of buoy)
			27177.1 / 39548.4 (1986)
			27176.9 / 39548.2 (1986)
1994	Concrete pipe: 246 pieces	34° 36.583' / 077° 02.183' to 34° 36.600' / 077° 02.183'	27176.9 / 39549.5 (1994 LORAN Concrete units added 19 Dec 86, 100-300' S to W of buoy)
		34° 36.617' / 077° 02.233'	27177.0 / 39549.5 (1994)
		34° 36.467' / 077° 02.167'	27177.1 / 39549.2 to 27177.1 / 39549.3
			27177.0 / 39549.1
16-Feb-83	Tire units: 19,488	34° 36.467' / 077° 02.167'	27176.8 / 39549.1
	Concrete pipe: 160 pieces	34° 36.583' / 077° 02.183'	
	Concrete pipe: 61 pieces	34° 36.550' / 077° 02.117'	
25-Feb-83	40 cu. ft. metal containers: 10 units		(site needs inspection to locate)

196

map continued on next page...

AR #342

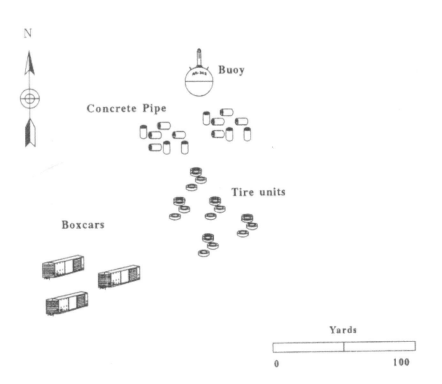

AR #345
Swansboro Rotary Club Reef

Range 143° magnetic — 8.1nm from Bogue Inlet sea buoy

Average Depth 60 feet

		GPS	LORAN
	Buoy	*34° 32.300' / 076° 58.467'	27160.2 / 39542.8

Deployment Date	Reef Material	GPS	LORAN
23-Dec-86	Box cars: 10	*34° 32.233' / 076° 58.500'	27160.5 / 39525.2
			27160.0 / 39524.5
			27160.2 / 39524.4
			27160.3 / 39523.6
			27160.6 / 39523.6
			27160.4 / 39523.9
1991	Concrete Pipe: 750 pieces	*34° 32.233' / 076° 58.417' to 34° 32.267' / 076° 58.450'	27160.1 / 39525.0 (East Group)
		34° 32.217' / 076° 58.383'	27159.8 / 39524.8
		34° 32.217' / 076° 58.417'	27160.0 / 39525.5
1991	Concrete pipe	*34° 32.300' / 076° 58.533'	27160.3 / 39525.3 (NW Group)
			27160.2 / 39524.8
	Concrete Vandoran units: 8	34° 32.400' / 076° 58.467' 34° 32.400' / 076° 58.483'	
3-Oct-00	Reef Balls: 75	34° 32.333' / 076° 58.333' to 34° 32.333' / 076° 58.367'	27159.8 / 39525.2 to 27159.9 / 39525.8
		34° 32.350' / 076° 58.317'	
		34° 32.333' / 076° 58.383'	

Additional Comments:

Box car LORAN's based original deployment location and need updating.

map continued on next page...

AR #345

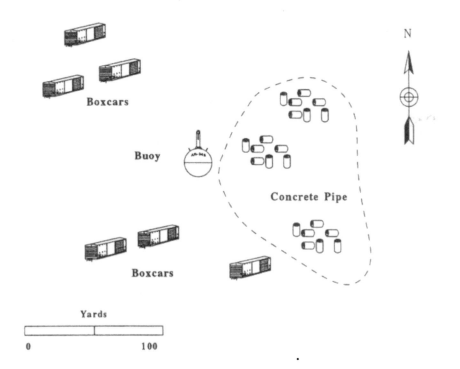

AR #350
New River Onslow County Reef

Average Depth 33 feet

		GPS	LORAN
	No Buoy		

Deployment Date	Reef Material	GPS	LORAN
2-Dec-75	Tires: 5,172	34° 29.800' / 077° 21.400'	27225.7 / 39404.2
14-Nov-84	80' Vessel	34° 29.800' / 077° 21.400'	27225.7 / 39404.2
23-Nov-87	10 Steel containers	34° 29.800' / 077° 21.400'	27225.7 / 39404.2

Additional Comments:

GPS and LORAN site locations only. Discontinued site due to live bottom.

AR #355
New River Reef

Range 185° magnetic — 9.7nm from Bogue Inlet sea buoy

Average Depth 60 feet

		GPS	LORAN
	Buoy	*34° 21.183' / 077° 20.000'	27210.0 / 39324.4

Deployment Date	Reef Material	GPS	LORAN
18-Dec-86	Box cars:10 (2 groups)	*34° 21.150' / 077° 19.983'	27210.1 / 39323.6 (150-400' SW of buoy) 27210.2 / 39323.7
1993	Hwy 172 Concrete bridge rubble	*34° 21.233' / 077° 19.900'	27209.6 / 39324.4
	10 barge loads	*34° 21.267' / 077° 19.967'	27209.8 / 39324.6
		*34° 21.283' / 077° 19.900'	27209.7 / 39324.8
		*34° 21.250' / 077° 19.983'	27210.1 / 39324.8
		*34° 21.200' / 077° 20.067'	27210.1 / 39324.1 to 27210.1 / 39323.9
		*34° 21.317' / 077° 19.983'	27209.9 / 39324.3
			27209.8 / 39324.3
			27210.0 / 39323.9
			27209.9 / 39323.9
			27210.2 / 39324.7
1993	60' ferro-cement vessel "SEA MINT"	*34° 21.200' / 077° 20.067'	27210.4 / 39323.2 to 27210.4 / 39323.3
	High Profile Units	34° 21.150' / 077° 20.983'	27209.9 / 39323.3

Additional Comments:

Box car, bridge rubble, barge load and "SEA MINT" are original LORAN deployment positions.

map continued on next page...

AR #355

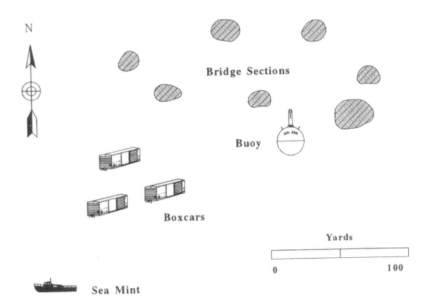

N

Bridge Sections

Buoy

Boxcars

Sea Mint

Yards

0   100

AR #360
Topsail Reef

Range 85° magnetic — 2.5nm from New Topsail Inlet sea buoy

Average Depth 44 feet

		GPS	LORAN
	Buoy	*34° 20.983' / 077° 36.183'	27256.9 / 39252.5

Deployment Date	Reef Material	GPS	LORAN
26-Sep-74	Tires - 48,700	Scattered around reef site, mostly buried	
1992	Concrete pipe 4' x 8': 850 pieces	*34° 21.017' / 077° 36.183'	27257.0 / 39252.6
		*34° 21.033' / 077° 36.200'	27257.1 / 39253.1

Additional Comments:

Concrete pipe pieces are original LORAN deployment positions.

map continued on next page...

AR #360

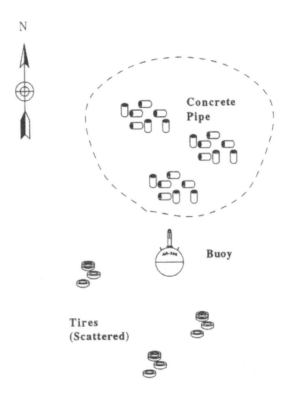

N

Concrete
Pipe

Buoy

Tires
(Scattered)

Yards

0   100

204

AR #362

Tom Boyette Reef

Range 126° magnetic — 8.7nm from New Topsail Inlet sea buoy

Average Depth 54 feet

		GPS	LORAN
	Buoy	*34° 15.717' / 077° 30.450'	27233.1 / 39224.5

Deployment Date	Reef Material	GPS	LORAN
5-Dec-86	Box cars - 10		27233.2 / 39223.4
			27233.1 / 39223.9
			27233.2 / 39223.0
1992	Concrete pipes:	*34° 15.767' / 077° 30.433'	27233.3 / 39224.3
	850 pieces 4' x 8'	*34° 15.733' / 077° 30.383'	27233.3 / 39224.0
		Above are original LORAN deployment positions	
		*34° 15.767' / 077° 30.417'	
		*34° 15.767' / 077° 30.383'	

map continued on next page...

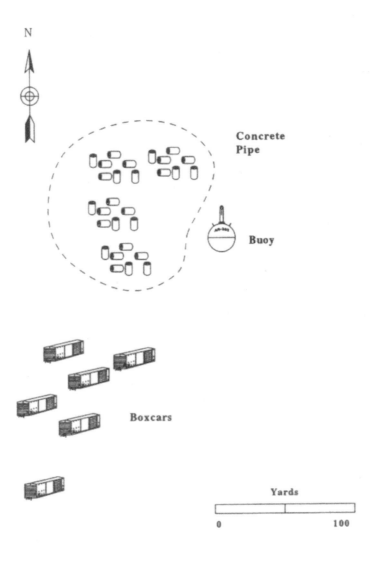

AR #364
Billy Murrell Reef

Range 050° magnetic — 6.2nm from Masonboro Inlet sea buoy

Average Depth 44 feet

		GPS	LORAN
	Buoy	*34° 14.833' / 077° 42.833'	27267.4 / 39160.6

Deployment Date	Reef Material	GPS	LORAN
1974-1984	Tires: 76,873	scattered on site	
18-Dec-86	32 Concrete pieces (480 tons)		(100-300' S of buoy)
12-May-88	65' tug 'SOUTHERN CRAFT 8'	*34° 14.850' / 077° 42.833'	27267.8 / 39161.6 (150' NW of buoy)
18-Jan-89	55' landing craft (LCM)	*34° 14.783' / 077° 42.850'	27267.5 / 39160.4
1990	Fiberglass Pre-fabricated Domes		27267.6 / 39162.6 (Original LORAN, needs update)
1992	52' tug 'CAPTAIN TOM'	*34° 14.833' / 077° 42.800'	27267.4 / 39161.4
1994	60' tug 'CAPTAIN JERRY'		27268.8 / 39161.3 (Original LORAN, needs update)
	298' barge - bow	*34° 14.767' / 077° 42.900'	
	298' barge - stern	*34° 14.817' / 077° 42.867'	

map continued on next page...

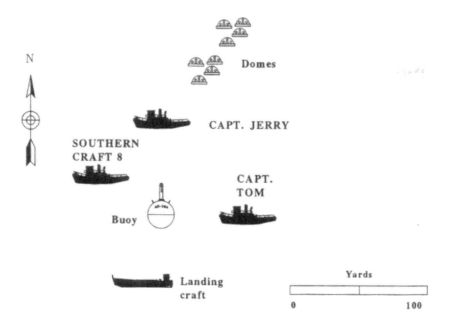

AR #366

Range 127° magnetic — 13.9nm from New Topsail Inlet sea buoy

Average Depth 60 feet

		GPS	LORAN
	Buoy	*34° 12.950' / 077° 25.250'	27214.6 / 39225.0

Deployment Date	Reef Material	GPS	LORAN
5-7 Dec-86	Box cars - 10		27214.7 / 39225.9
			(300-800' SW of buoy)
			27214.7 / 39224.0
1992	Concrete pipe 4' x 8': 850 pieces	*34° 12.983' / 077° 25.267'	27214.7 / 39224.9
		*34° 12.950' / 077° 25.233'	27214.7 / 39225.3
			27214.7 / 39225.5

Additional Comments:

Box cars are original LORAN, need updates

map continued on next page...

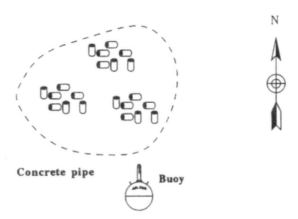

N

Concrete pipe

Buoy

Boxcars

Yards

0   100

AR #368

Range 140° magnetic — 15.5nm from New Topsail Inlet sea buoy

Average Depth 66 feet

		GPS	LORAN
	Buoy	*34° 09.567' / 077° 25.833'	27211.7 / 39195.0

Deployment Date	Reef Material	GPS	LORAN
7-Dec-86	Box cars - 10	*34° 09.417' / 077° 25.917'	27211.9 / 39193.6 (300-700' SW of buoy)
			27214.8 / 39193.9
1994	241' barge 'LC-16'	*34° 09.583' / 077° 25.917'	27211.6 / 39195.6
			27211.8 / 39195.5
	Scattered rubble	*34° 09.583' / 077° 25.933'	
		*34° 09.583' / 077° 25.883'	
		*34° 09.567' / 077° 25.967'	

map continued on next page...

AR #368

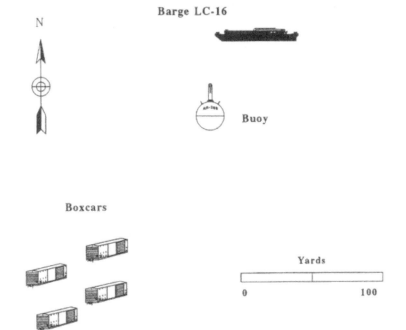

Barge LC-16

N

Buoy

Boxcars

Yards

0   100

AR #370
Meares Harris Reef

Range 100° magnetic — 3.5nm from Masonboro Inlet sea buoy

Average Depth 52 feet

		GPS	LORAN
	Buoy	*34° 10.467' / 077° 45.067'	27267.8 / 39106.3

Deployment Date	Reef Material	GPS	LORAN
1-Aug-73	(2) 90' barges	*34° 10.467' / 077° 44.800'	27267.0 / 39108.4
			27267.1 / 39107.2
26-Aug-74	440' liberty ship "ALEXANDER RAMSEY"	*34° 10.517' / 077° 45.117'	27268.0 / 39106.4
25-Sep-80	135' x 30' x 18' barge	*34° 10.483' / 077° 44.783'	27267.0 / 39107.6
15-Dec-82	120' tug "SICONY 8"	*34° 10.533' / 077° 45.083'	
2-Jun-70	110' tug		27267.3 / 39107.2
14-Jan-83	105' tug "STONE BROTHERS"		27266.5 / 39106.5
Summer 1972	50' tanker		
1973 - 1974	Tires: 56,500	Probably scattered throughout and possibly buried	

map continued on next page...

AR #370

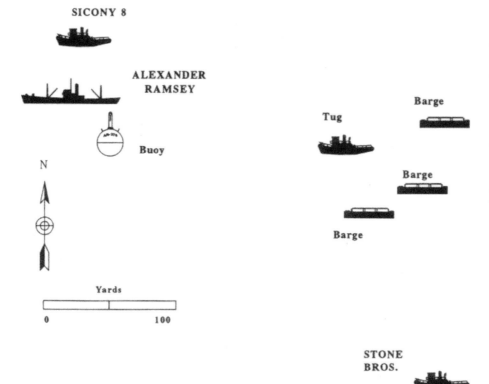

AR #372

Range 100° magnetic — 3.5nm from Masonboro Inlet sea buoy

Average Depth 48 feet

		GPS	LORAN
	Buoy	*34° 06.217' / 077° 44.950'	27261.4 / 39068.9

Deployment Date	Reef Material	GPS	LORAN
7-Nov-86	Box cars - 10		27261.3 / 39068.1 (100-500'SW of buoy)
1990	220' barge (Northern)	*34°06.250' / 077° 44.800'	27261.0 / 39069.3 (one barge with boat mold)
1990	220' barge (Southern)	*34° 06.233' / 077° 44.800'	27261.1 / 39068.9

map continued on next page...

AR #372

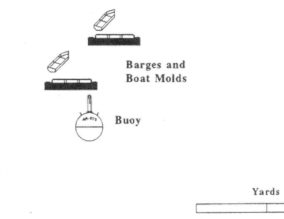

N

Barges and
Boat Molds

Buoy

Yards

0   100

Boxcars

216

AR #376

Range 142° magnetic — 9.9nm from Masonboro Inlet sea buoy

Average Depth 60 feet

		GPS	LORAN
Buoy		*34° 03.283' / 077°39.633'	27243.1 / 39077.2

Deployment Date	Reef Material	GPS	LORAN
1986	Box cars - 10 total	*34° 03.267' / 077° 39.617'	27242.8 / 39077.1
	(2 groups of 5)		(5-100-500' NE of buoy)
			27242.8 / 39076.6
			(5-100-400' SW of buoy)
			27243.2 / 39076.0
			to
			27243.2 / 39076.2
			27243.1 / 39077.1
			27242.7 / 39078.3
1992	Concrete pipe	*34° 03.333' / 077° 39.700'	27243.4 / 39077.4
	5' x 8': 850 pieces		27243.4 / 39077.6
			27243.6 / 39078.0
			27243.7 / 39077.7
			27243.4 / 39077.8
	Concrete	34° 03.267' / 077° 39.583'	27242.9 / 39078.9
	VanDoren units: 7		to
			2742.8 / 39078.1
		34° 03.267' / 077° 39.616'	

map continued on next page...

AR #376

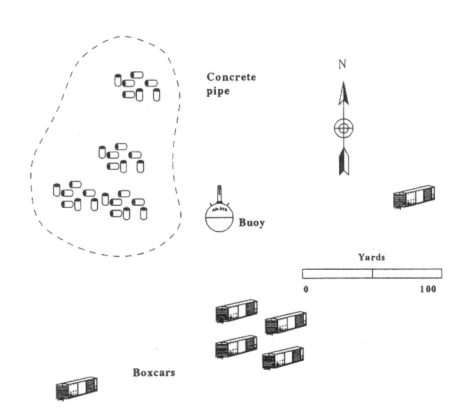

AR #378
Philip Wolfe Reef

Range 184° magnetic — 2.6nm from Carolina Beach Inlet

208° magnetic — 8.9nm from Masonboro Inlet

Average Depth 40 feet

	GPS	LORAN
Buoy		(9960) 27275.5 / 57509.2
		(7980) 45336.0 / 58990.4

Deployment Date	Reef Material	GPS	LORAN
5-May-82	98' barges: 3	34° 00.633' / 077° 50.683'	27275.6 / 57509.6
			27270.2 / 57513.4
5-May-82	Tires: 111,000	34° 00.783' / 077° 50.667'	(Probably scattered throughout reef site or buried)
1993	195' barge	34° 01.817' / 077° 52.133'	27275.6 / 57502.2
1999	Concrete Pipe: 134 pieces	34° 01.850' / 077° 52.267 to 34° 01.817' / 077° 52.300'	
2001	Reef Balls: 25	34° 01.783' / 077° 52.233'	NE unit
2001	Reef Balls: 25	34° 01.783' / 077° 52.250'	NW unit
2001	Reef Balls: 25	34° 01.767' / 077° 52.250'	SE unit
2001	Reef Balls: 25	34° 01.767' / 077° 52.233'	SW unit

map continued on next page...

AR #378

Buoy

N

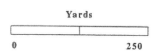

Yards

0   250

Tires
(Scattered)

Barge

220

AR #382

Dredge Wreck Reef

Range 130° magnetic — 10.7nm from Carolina Beach Inlet sea buoy

160 magnetic — 13.0 nm from Masonboro Inslet sea buoy

Average Depth 58 feet

		GPS	LORAN
Buoy		*33° 58.583' / 077° 41.283'	27241.5 / 39047.0

Deployment Date	Reef Material	GPS	LORAN
early 1940's	Dredge Wreck	*33° 58.500' / 077° 41.283'	27241.2 / 39046.7
26-Feb-85	105' tug 'POCAHONTAS'	33° 58.583' / 077° 40.917'	27240.6 / 39048.3
27-Feb-85	86' tug 'R.R. STONE'	33° 58.467' / 077° 41.283'	27241.6 / 39046.0
2001	Reef Balls	33° 58.483' / 077° 41.283'	East end
2001	Reef Balls	33° 58.467' / 077° 41.383'	West end

map continued on next page...

AR #382

N

 Buoy

R.R.
STONE

POCAHONTAS

Dredge
Wreck

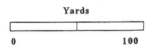

Yards

0   100

222

AR #386
Lennon/Hyde Reef

Range 143° magnetic — 17.8nm from Masonboro Inlet sea buoy

Average Depth 78 feet

		GPS	LORAN
	Buoy	*33° 57.517' / 077° 33.450'	27218.3 / 39082.2

Deployment Date	Reef Material	GPS	LORAN
29-Oct-86	Box cars: 10		27217.5 / 39082.4
			27217.6 / 39082.5
			27217.6 / 39082.4
			27217.5 / 39082.5
			27217.6 / 39082.7
			27217.4 / 39082.6
			27217.7 / 39082.7
22-Oct-87	150' YTT barge (schoolhouse) "ALTON LENNON"	*33° 57.633' / 077° 33.400'	27218.3 / 39082.7
20-May-88	215' dredge "HYDE"	*33° 57.450' / 077° 33.433'	27218.1 / 39081.9
	320' dredge "MARKHAM"	*33° 57.633' / 077° 33.200'	

map continued on next page...

223

AR #386

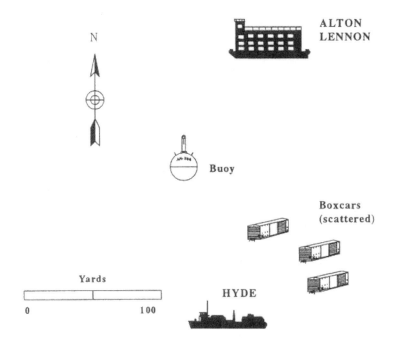

AR #400
Frying pan Light Station Reef

Average Depth 48-70 feet

		GPS	LORAN
	No Buoy on this site		

Deployment Date	Reef Material	GPS	LORAN
1964	Tower legs	33°28.15'/077°35.25'	45166.3/59220.5
Jul-04	Tower super structure	33°29.27'/077°35.25'	

Additional Comments

Frying Pan Light Station is located about 35 miles southeast of Cape Fear. AR 400 will be located 1/4 mile northeast of the current tower's location. The tower legs will be cut 24 feet below the surface to provide safe clearance for ships. There will be no buoy marking the location of the current site or location of the new reef.

The tower material will be cleaned and submerged over an area approximately 175' by 210' at coordinates 33 degrees 29.27minutes North; 77 degrees, 35.25 minutes West. Besides the tower, other material such as vessels, concrete pipe or artificial attractors called reef balls could be added to the site in the future. The entire site is designated as AR 400 is approximately one-half mile in diameter to allow for expansion. The remnants will be placed in the center. The current tower location is within the southwestern quadrant of the AR 400 site.

AR #420

Tom McGlammery Reef

Range 315° magnetic — 3.0nm from Cape Fear River sea buoy

Average Depth 30 feet

		GPS	LORAN
Buoy		*33° 50.400' / 078° 07.233'	45347.9 / 59184.8

Deployment Date	**Reef Material**	**GPS**	**LORAN**
6-Sept-86	104' YSD barge	33° 51.084' / 078° 06.630'	45348.0 / 59184.5 to 45348.2 / 59184.6
3-Jan-87	180' barge HT-85	33° 51.150' / 078° 06.567'	(200' south of buoy)
3-Jan-87	230' bridge span	33° 51.066' / 078° 06.678'	45348.1 / 59185.0
1992	Concrete pipe and manhole sections: 60 pieces	33° 51.033' / 078° 06.650'	45348.0 / 59185.0 to 45348.0 / 59185.1 45348.7 / 59183.6 45348.4 / 59184.7
Mar-00	Potter Barge	33° 50.975' / 078° 06.691'	45347.8 / 59185.7
Apr-00	Reef Balls: 50	33° 51.013' / 078° 06.618' 33° 51.000' / 078° 06.617'	45347.6 / 59185.2 45347.7 / 59185.2
23-Mar-01	Concrete pipe: 62 pieces, 36" x 8'	33° 50.966' / 078° 06.810' All in one pile 15' relief	
26-Mar-01	Concrete pipe: 61 pieces, 36" x 8'	33° 50.952' / 078° 06.802' All in one pile 15' relief	
9-Apr-00	Concrete pipe: 15 pieces, 36" x 8' All in one pile 15' relief		
2000	Reef Balls: 50	33° 51.013' / 078° 06.618'	

AR #420 continued

Deployment Date	Reef Material	GPS	LORAN
Winter 2001	Reef Balls: 25	33° 53.150' / 078° 06.600'	
	Reef Balls: 25	33° 53.167' / 078° 06.567'	
	Reef Balls: 25	33° 53.150' / 078° 06.550'	
	Reef Balls: 25	33° 53.133' / 078° 06.583'	
Winter 2001	Concrete pipe	33° 53.017' / 078° 06.617'	
		33° 53.000' / 078° 06.633'	
		33° 53.017' / 078° 06.600'	
		33° 52.983' / 078° 06.617'	

Additional Comments:

All 400 series reef locations are given in LORAN Chain (GRI) 7980 unless otherwise noted.

map continued on next page...

AR #420

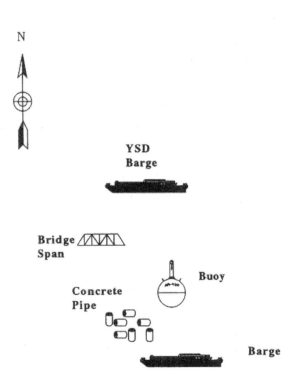

N

YSD
Barge

Bridge
Span

Concrete
Pipe

Buoy

Barge

AR #425
Yaupon Beach Reef

Range 315° magnetic — 3.0nm from Cape Fear River sea buoy

Average Depth 30 feet

		GPS	LORAN
	Buoy	*33° 53.050' / 078° 06.567'	45354.7 / 59169.6

Deployment Date	Reef Material	GPS	LORAN
1987	600 tons concrete rubble	(100-300' SW of buoy)	
1989	Bridge railing: 100 pieces	33° 53.067' / 078° 06.517'	45354.5 / 59169.1
		*33° 53.050' / 078° 06.483'	45354.3 / 59169.1
		*33° 53.067' / 078° 06.483'	45354.5 / 59168.9
Unknown	Unknown Barge	33° 53.068 / 078° 14.062'	
1992	Concrete pipe/ manhole sections: 240 pieces	33° 53.004' / 078° 06.653'	45354.4 / 59169.7
1993, 1994	Concrete pipe	*33° 52.998' / 078° 06.523'	45354.7 / 59169.2
		*33° 53.062' / 078° 06.516'	45354.7 / 59170.2
		*33° 53.100' / 078° 06.567'	45354.9 / 59169.7
		*33° 53.033' / 078° 06.567'	
	Concrete Vandoren units: 8	33° 53.067' / 078° 06.617'	
		33° 53.033' / 078° 06.617'	
2000	Reef Balls: 33	33° 52.983' / 078° 06.567'	
	Reef Balls: 33	33° 53.100' / 078° 06.500'	
	Reef Balls: 33	33° 53.033' / 078° 06.083'	

continued

Deployment Date	Reef Material	GPS	LORAN
Mar-00	Reef Balls: 25	33° 53.167' / 078° 06.583'	North section
	Reef Balls: 25	33° 53.150' / 078° 06.550'	East section
	Reef Balls: 25	33° 53.133' / 078° 06.583'	South section
	Reef Balls: 25	33° 53.150' / 078° 06.600'	West section
Mar-00	Reef Balls	33° 53.103' / 078° 06.614'	45355.2 / 59169.9
		33° 52.975' / 078° 06.567'	45354.5 / 59170.3
Feb-01	Concrete pipe: 147 pieces	33° 53.015' / 078° 06.621' to 33° 53.004' / 078° 06.610'	
14-Mar-01	Concrete pipe: 62 pieces, 4 x 4		
Winter 2001	Concrete pipe	33° 50.967' / 078° 06.817'	
		33° 50.967' / 078° 06.800'	
		33° 50.950' / 078° 06.817'	
Winter 2001	Concrete pipe	33° 53.017' / 078° 06.617'	
		33° 53.000' / 078° 06.633'	
		33° 53.017' / 078° 06.600'	
		33° 52.983' / 078° 06.617'	

Additional Comments:

All 400 series reef locations are given in LORAN Chain (GRI) 7980 unless otherwise noted.

map continued on next page...

AR #425

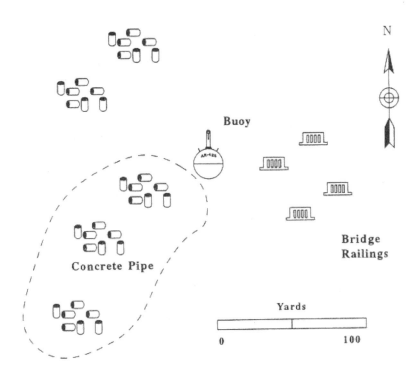

Buoy

Concrete Pipe

Bridge
Railings

N

Yards

0   100

AR #440
Brunswick County Fishing Club Reefs

Range 169° magnetic — 4.5nm from Lockwood's Folly Inlet sea buoy.

279° magnetic — 7.6nm from Cape Fear River sea buoy.

Average Depth 42 feet

		GPS	LORAN
	Buoy	*33° 49.800' / 078° 13.083'	43365.8 / 59246.6

Deployment Date	Reef Material	GPS	LORAN
1987	Box cars: 7	200 - 600' SSW of the buoy	
1987	Boiler pieces: 4	33° 49.767' / 078° 13.050' (200 - 300' SE to SW of bouy)	45365.6 / 59246.8
1987			45365.4 / 59247.0
1987			45365.6 / 59246.4
1992-1993	Concrete pipe: 150 pieces in 1992	33° 49.817' / 078° 13.100'	27316.5 / 57390.5 (9960)
		33° 49.833' / 078° 13.083'	27316.5 / 57390.5
			45365.8 / 59246.7
	Concrete: 60 tons: 4 pieces	200' East of bouy	
1993	65' tug "A.T. PINER"	*33° 49.800' / 078° 13.100'	45365.8 / 59246.7
1993	65' tug "COOPEDGE"	33° 49.800' / 078° 13.100'	45366.0 / 59246.9
Apr-00	Reef Balls:(100)	33° 49.767' / 078° 13.017'	45365.5 / 59246.4
	3 groups	33° 49.767' / 078° 13.100'	45365.6 / 59247.1
		33° 49.767' / 078° 13.583'	45365.3 / 59246.7
20-Feb-01	Concrete pipe: 104 pieces		

AR #440 continued

Deployment Date	Reef Material	GPS	LORAN
21-Feb-01	Concrete pipe: 100 pieces		
4-Apr-01	Concrete pipe: 105 pieces 30"		
5-Apr-01	Concrete pipe: 105 pieces 30"		
1987	Boiler Pieces	34° 49.776' / 078° 13.093'	
1987	Boiler Pieces	34° 49.803 / 078° 13.067	

map continued on next page...

AR #440

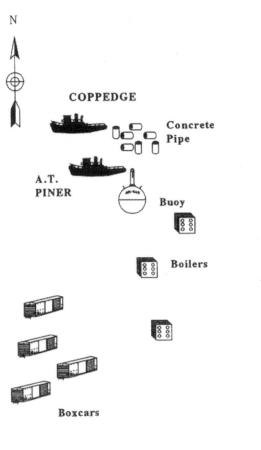

N

COPPEDGE

Concrete
Pipe

A.T.
PINER

Buoy

Boilers

Boxcars

AR #445

Range 185° magnetic — 9.3nm from Lockwood's Folly Inlet sea buoy

Average Depth 53 feet

		GPS	LORAN
	Buoy	*33° 44.783' / 078° 14.100'	45352.0 / 59289.0

Deployment Date	Reef Material	GPS	LORAN
1986	Box cars: 10	100 - 800' SE to SW of buoy	
1991	174' vessel "JELL II"	*33° 44.850' / 078° 14.050'	
		*33° 44.833' / 078° 14.067'	
1991	Fiberglass and steel boat molds: 100		45352.4 / 59291.4
			to
			45352.3 / 59291.4
			45352.5 / 59291.2
			45352.4 / 59291.1
			45352.6 / 59291.4
			45351.8 / 59287.3
			to
			45351.8 / 59287.4
1993	Concrete sections		45351.9 / 59289.7
1994	Concrete pipe: 250 pieces	*33° 44.767' / 078° 14.033'	45351.3 / 59289.5
		*33° 44.750' / 078° 14.083'	45351.2 / 59290.3
			45351.5 / 59289.5
			45351.4 / 59290.0
Apr-00	Reef Balls: 100	33° 44.767' / 078° 14.167'	45352.5 / 59291.4
		33° 44.800' / 078° 14.267'	45352.6 / 59291.4
		33° 44.867' / 078° 14.350'	45352.0 / 59289.1
27-Feb-01	Concrete pipe: 182 pieces		

continued

Deployment Date	Reef Material	GPS	LORAN
12-Mar-01	Concrete pipe: 135 pieces		
Winter 2001	Concrete pipe	33° 44.867' / 078° 14.200'	
		33° 44.850' / 078° 14.200'	
		33° 44.867' / 078° 14.183'	
		33° 44.883' / 078° 14.150'	
		33° 44.867' / 078° 14.167'	

map continued on next page...

AR #445

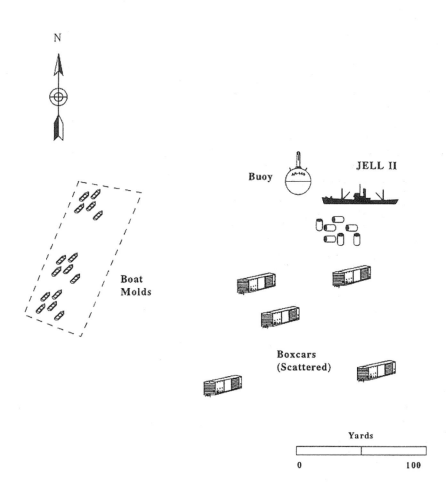

N

Buoy

JELL II

Boat
Molds

Boxcars
(Scattered)

Yards

0   100

AR #455

Range 156° magnetic — 7.0nm from Shallotte Inlet sea buoy.

265° magnetic — 12.2nm from Cape Fear River sea buoy.

Average Depth 46 feet

		GPS	LORAN
	Buoy	*33° 47.033' / 078° 17.883'	45373.0 / 59306.0

Deployment Date	Reef Material	GPS	LORAN
24-27 Oct-86	Box cars: 10		45372.6 / 59305.8
			(200 - 600' SE to SW of buoy)
			45372.4 / 59305.6
			45372.6 / 59306.1
1992, 1993	Concrete pipe: 300 pieces in 1993	*33° 47.083' / 078° 17.933'	45373.1 / 59305.9
		*33° 47.050' / 078° 17.900'	45372.9 / 59305.8
			45372.8 / 59306.0
			45373.1 / 59305.9
			45372.9 / 59305.8
			45372.7 / 59305.4
1992	Concrete manhole sections: 150 pieces		45372.7 / 59305.4
Apr-01	Reef Balls: 100	33° 47.000' / 078° 17.950'	NE section
		33° 46.967' / 078° 17.933'	SE section
		33° 46.967' / 078° 17.983'	SW section
		33° 46.983' / 078° 17.983'	NW section
		33° 50.183' / 078° 22.100'	
	Reef Balls: 100	33° 47.000' / 078° 17.867'	45372.6 / 59306.0
		33° 47.033' / 078° 17.900'	45372.7 / 59306.1
		33° 47.050' / 078° 17.933'	45372.7 / 59306.2
27-Mar-01	Concrete pipe: 65 pieces - 36" x 8'	33° 47.033' / 078° 17.783'	
28-Mar-01	Concrete pipe: 30 pieces - 30" x 8',	33° 47.000' / 078° 17.767'	
	Concrete pipe: 44 pieces - 36" x 8'		
16-Apr-01	Concrete pipe: 230 pieces	33° 47.017' / 078° 17.800'	
		33° 47.000' / 078° 17.800'	

AR #455 continued

Deployment Date	Reef Material	GPS	LORAN
Winter 2001	Concrete pipe	33° 47.033' / 078° 17.783'	
		33° 47.017' / 078° 17.783'	
		33° 47.017' / 078° 17.800'	
		33° 47.000' / 078° 17.783'	
		33° 47.000' / 078° 17.800'	
Winter 2001	Reef Balls	33° 46.983' / 078° 17.983'	
		33° 46.950' / 078° 17.983'	
		33° 47.000' / 078° 17.933'	
		33° 46.967' / 078° 17.933'	

map continued on next page...

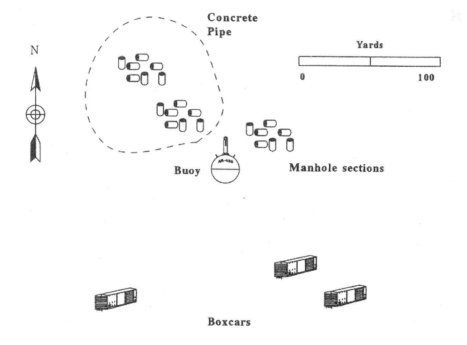

AR #460

Range 183° magnetic — 3.0nm from Shallotte Inlet sea buoy

Average Depth 38 feet

		GPS	LORAN
	Buoy	*33° 50.217' / 078° 22.033'	45398.0 / 59323.0

Deployment Date	Reef Material	GPS	LORAN
1986	Box Cars: 10	100 - 500' SE to NW of buoy	
1990 (9960)	330' barge	33° 50.133' / 078° 21.933'	27340.7 / 57350.1
Apr-01	Reef Balls: 100	33° 50.267' / 078° 22.050'	NW section
		33° 50.267' / 078° 22.000'	NE section
		33° 50.233' / 078° 22.000'	SE section
		33° 50.233' / 078° 22.050'	SW section
		33° 50.200' / 078° 21.967'	45398.2 / 59322.7
		33° 50.150' / 078° 21.983'	45397.8 / 59322.8
		33° 50.167' / 078° 21.017'	45398.0 / 59323.0
28-Feb-01	Concrete pipe - 126 pieces	33° 50.183' / 078° 22.100'	
3-Apr-01	Concrete pipe - 105 pieces - 30' x 8'		
Winter 2001	Concrete pipe	33° 50.183' / 078° 22.083'	
		33° 50.167' / 078° 22.083'	
		33° 50.183' / 078° 22.133'	
		33° 50.183' / 078° 22.100'	
		33° 50.167' / 078° 22.100'	
		33° 50.167' / 078° 22.133'	
		33° 50.150' / 078° 22.133'	

map continued on next page...

AR #460

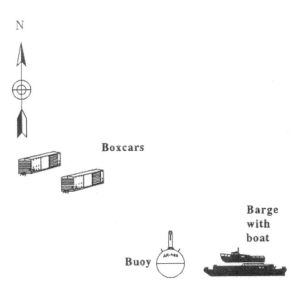

N

Boxcars

Barge
with
boat

Buoy

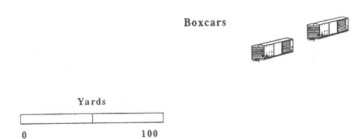

Boxcars

Yards

0   100

AR #465

		GPS	LORAN
Average Depth 90 feet			
	No Buoy		

Deployment Date	Reef Material	GPS	LORAN
	180' vessel "MANCE LASSITER"	*33° 23.417' / 078° 11.050'	
		*33° 23.400' / 078° 11.067'	
	Ultra Reef Balls: 100	33° 23.417' / 078° 11.000'	N section
		33° 23.350' / 078° 11.000'	S section
		33° 23.383' / 078° 10.983'	W section
		33° 23.383' / 078° 10.017'	E section
	Reef Balls: 2 areas of 50 units	33° 23.382' / 078° 11.070' and 33° 23.416' / 078° 11.166'	

Estuarine Reefs

Reef:	**AR-191-Black Walnut Point Reef**
Location:	140° magnetic from marker 2 at entrance to Edenton Channel, 1.0 NM due north of Black Walnut Point
Material:	220 tires; 12 boat molds (donated by Fiberform Boat Company, Edenton, NC); 10 - 40 cu ft trash boxes; Deployment date 1-Oct-84
GPS:	36° 00.000' / 076° 40.000'

Reef:	**AR-291 Bayview Reef (Pamlico River)**
Location:	100' offshore Town of Bayview, near the mouth of Bath Creek; Average Depth 17 feet
Material:	28,180 tires
GPS:	35° 25.917' / 076° 45.700'

Reef:	**AR-292 Quilley Point (Pungo River)**
Location:	90° magnetic - 0.75 nm from ICW marker #5; Average Depth 14 feet
Materials:	19,200 tires; Mail boxes
GPS:	35° 28.250' / 076° 34.250'

Reef:	**AR-296 Hatteras Island Business Association Reef**
Location:	1.0 nm north of Frisco Channel marker #6; Buoy LORAN 26950.0 / 40280.0
Materials:	Tires; 1 group marl rock; Deployment date 1-Mar-85 Marl rock Class B Rip Rap (Six mounds)
GPS:	35° 17.333' / 075° 37.500'
	35°17.418 / 075° 37.374' (mound 1)
	35°17.427 / 075° 37.285' (mound 2)
	35°17.341 / 075° 37.349' (mound 3)
	35°17.337 / 075° 37.282' (mound 4)
	35°17.249 / 075° 37.296' (mound 5)
	35°17.271 / 075° 37.235' (mound 6)

Reef:	**AR-391**

Estuarine Reefs continued

Materials:	Tires: 10,440; Deployment date 1-Oct-84
GPS:	Permit expired 31-Dec-86

Reef:	AR-392 New Bern (Neuse River)
Location:	140° magnetic – 2.6nm from Union Point Park, Neuse River; Buoy LORAN 27211.2 / 29858.9; Average Depth 13–15 feet
Materials:	104,760 Tires; Deployment dates 1984-1985
GPS:	n/a

Reef:	**AR-396 Oriental (Neuse River)**
Location:	900 yards SE of Whitehurst Point near Oriental; Average Depth 11–15 feet
Materials:	21,820 tires; barge load scrap material; Fossil rock (marl) Deployment dates 1973-1985
GPS:	35° 01.833' / 076° 39.500'

246

Glossary of Terms

Glossary

Amberjack, Greater (*Seriola Dumerili*)—A game fish with a dark oblique line beginning at the eye and ending at the tail. The fish is a strong fighter that digs deep. Common weights are 10 to 60 pounds. World Record is 155 pounds, 12 ounces. Also called A.J., amber fish or rubber lip.

Anchovy (*Anchoa sp.*)—Any of several species of small minnows that are important forage fish for game fish. Also called glass minnows.

Bonito, Atlantic (*Sarda sarda*)—A game fish identified by horizontal dark stripes on the upper half of the body. The fish is a strong fighter that swims in large schools. Common weights are 4 to 10 pounds. World record is 18 pounds, 4 ounces. Also called striped bonito, striped ape, Boston mackerel and common bonito.

Ballyhoo (*Hemiramphus brasiliensis*)—An important baitfish characterized by a long beak extending from the lower jaw. Also called balao and half-beak.

Barracuda, Great (*Sphyraena barracuda*)—A game fish with jagged teeth and a pointed head, also characterized by dark blotches on its sides. Barracuda fight with long, fast runs and high leaps. Common weights are 10 to 30 pounds. World record is 84 pounds, 14 ounces. Also called sea pike or 'cuda.

Barrel Wrap—A style of knot used in tying single-strand wire leaders consisting of tight wraps around the standing part that touch one another.

Biomass—The combined animal and plant life an area can support.

Black Sea Bass (*Centropristis striata*)—A game fish with an overall black appearance caught in deep ocean waters. Black sea bass provide a strong fight on light tackle and are excellent to eat. Common weights are 1 to 4 pounds. World record is 9 pounds, 12 ounces. Also called blackfish.

Blood Worm—A burrowing worm that is dug from the estuaries of the Northeast and sent to the nation's coastal fishing tackle and bait stores for use as bait by anglers.

Bluefish (*Pomatomus saltatrix*)—A game fish with steel-blue sides, often with a black spot below the dorsal fin. Bluefish have powerful jaws and sharp teeth and fight hard, often leaping from the water when hooked. Common weights are 1 to 10 pounds. World record is 31 pounds, 12 ounces. Also called tailors, snappers, choppers.

Boston Mackerel (*Scomber japonicus*)—An important baitfish that is caught north of Cape Hatteras, primarily in northern states and can be purchased frozen for use as fishing bait. Also called tinker, hard head and chub mackerel.

Cha-Raider—Trade name for a minnow-imitating lure molded of Nylon that can be cast, trolled or jigged (*Barefoot Baits*, Wilmington, NC).

Chopper Bluefish—A large bluefish.

Chum—Ground fish, oil, pet food or livestock feed that anglers place into the water to attract and concentrate game fish.

Cigar Minnow (*Decapterus punctatus*)—A cigar-shaped baitfish that can be caught in ocean waters with multiple gold-hook rigs or cast nets and is also purchased frozen from bait and tackle shops. The more accurate common name for the fish is round scad.

Circle Hook—A style of hook originally used by commercial anglers setting longlines and adapted by offshore anglers for some game fish species. The hook shank and point nearly touch or overlap. The design of circle hooks helps prevent gut-hooked fish and allows fish to hook themselves in the corner of the jaws.

Clarkspoon—Trade name for a style of metal trolling lure (*James E. Clark, Inc.*, St. Petersburg, FL).

Cobia (*Rachycentron canadum*)—A long-bodied game fish with dark brown, leathery skin, a flat head, and a dark line extending along the flanks from gills to tail that is especially prominent in smaller fish. Powerful fighters, cobia make strong runs and have lots of stamina. Common weights are 20 to 50 pounds but certain specimens can be much larger. World record is 135 pounds, 9 ounces.

Color Scope—An electronic sonar device that shows varying strengths of return signals in different colors. Also called a color depthfinder or color machine.

Crab, Blue (*Callinctes sapidus*)—An edible crustacean with four pairs of legs and one pair of claws. Blue crabs make great baits for some game fish.

Cuddy Cabin—A protected area that is located in the bow of a boat and can contain washroom and sleeping facilities.

Diamond Jig—Trade name for a style of lure with a metal body that is square or diamond shaped in cross section and is used for jigging. (*Bead Tackle, Inc.*, Pawtucket, RI).

Dolphin (*Coryphaena hippurus*)—A colorful game fish with a blue or green and bright yellow body. Males (bulls) have high, blunted foreheads while females (cows) have rounded foreheads.

The fish combines long, stubborn runs with high leaps when hooked and is among the most desirable fish sought by offshore anglers. Common weights are 1 to 20 pounds, but often up to 50 pounds. World record is 88 pounds.

Doors—Metal-bound wooden diving planes that guide a shrimp trawl along the bottom of the ocean floor and keep the net open.

Downrigger—An electronic or mechanical device consisting of a winch mechanism, cable, line or wire, and a weight or planer that is used to carry a bait or lure beneath the water surface. In sport fishing, a release clip is used to free the line and allow the fish to be played with a rod and reel.

Drone Spoon—Trade name for a style of metal trolling lure (*L. B. Huntington*, Norfolk, VA).

Dropper Loop—A style of knot used to tie a hook above a weight or lure rather than at the end of the line or leader.

EPIRB—Stands for Emergency Position Indicating Radio Beacon. When activated, it emits an emergency signal that is picked up by satellites and transmitted via land-based receivers to the U.S. Coast Guard. EPIRBs are a last resort measure for emergency use only.

False Albacore (*Euthynnus alletteratus*)—A game fish that is rich blue above and silvery below with a wavy pattern on the upper side, behind the dorsal fin, and spots near the pectoral fin. The fish is a strong fighter with lots of endurance when hooked on light tackle. Most anglers don't eat false albacore, but the fish is often retained to make Gulf Stream trolling baits. Common weights are 1 to 10 pounds but can exceed 30 pounds. World record is 35 pounds, 2 ounces. Also called spotted bonito, Fat Albert, Florida Bonito, Little Tunny.

251

Flatline—A line from a rod that is set near the transom of the boat without the use of an outrigger or downrigger. A release clip, connected to the reel, rod butt or stern is used to hold the line down near the water surface during windy or choppy conditions.

Flounder (*Summer-Paralichthys dentatus; Southern–P. lethostigma*)—A flat-bodied fish with both eyes on the dorsal side. Summer flounder and southern flounder are difficult to differentiate by untrained anglers. The body is dark above and white below. The fish is a good fighter on light tackle and highly sought for the table. Common weights are 2 to 4 pounds but can reach up to 10 pounds. World record for summer flounder is 22 pounds, 7 ounces and for southern flounder, 20 pounds, 9 ounces. Also called flatfish, fluke, doormat, flattie.

Fluorocarbon—A type of monofilament leader material that is nearly invisible in the water and very resistant to abrasion.

Fly Net—A large trawl used by commercial fishermen to catch fish from the ocean. Fly nets were partly blamed for the crash of the weakfish population because of the juvenile fish caught and discarded as bycatch. Fly nets are now highly regulated.

Flying fish–(*Exocoetus sp., Cypselurus sp., Hirundichthys sp.*)— Flying fish leap from the water and fly for long distances when startled by a boat or pursued by predators. Because the flying fish is primary forage fish for dolphin, the presence of flying fish is an indication that dolphin may be in the vicinity.

Gibbs Minnow—Trade name for a type of heavy metal lure that is usually jigged up and down to attract fish (*Gibbs Nortac*, Burnsby, B.C., Canada).

Glass Minnow—Translucent or transparent minnows, usually anchovy species.

GPS—Stands for Global Positioning System. GPS is a satellite-based radio-navigation system developed and operated by the U.S. Department of Defense. It permits land, sea and air users to determine their three-dimensional position, velocity and time anywhere in the world. GPS signals are becoming more accurate for civilian use and will probably supplant Loran-C at some point.

Grouper (Black–*Mycteroperca bonaci*; Gag–*M. microlepis*; Scamp–*M. phenax*; Jewfish–*Epinephelus itajara*; Nassau–*E. striatus*; Red-*E. morio*; Red Hind-*E. guttatus*; Rock Hind–*E. adscensionis*; Snowy–*E. niveatus*; Speckled Hind–*E. drummondhayi*; Warsaw–*E. nigritus*)—A group of fish that are often highly colorful or have distinct dark patterns with large mouths and stout bodies. Grouper are strong fighters, even on heavy bottom-fishing gear, and are highly sought by offshore anglers. Common weights are 1 to 30 pounds with some species larger and some smaller. World records are: Black–114 pounds; Gag–80 pounds, 6 ounces; Jewfish-680 pounds; Nassau–38 pounds, 8 ounces; Red–42 pounds, 4 ounces; Red Hind–6 pounds, 1 ounce; Rock Hind–9 pounds; Scamp–29 pounds; Snowy–23 pounds; Speckled Hind–52 pounds, 8 ounces; Warsaw–436 pounds, 12 ounces. An incredible number of common names exist for the various grouper species. Some other species common to more tropical waters may occur incidentally off the Carolina coast. Anglers must learn to identify species by the names used by regulatory agencies because size and creel limits and prohibitions against possession exist for individual grouper species. The Jewfish was officially renamed the Goliath Grouper in 2001.

Grunt–(Tomtate–*Haemolun aurolineatum*; White Grunt–*H. Plumieri*; Margate–*H. album*; Bluetriped Grunt–*H. sciurus*; French Grunt–*Haemuluon flavolineatum*; Black Margate–*Anistostremus surinamensis*)—Grunts are caught while bottom fishing for grouper and snapper. The grunting sounds of the fish are made by their internal organs. The most important grunt in Carolina waters is the white grunt, also called the gray grunt, which commonly weighs up to 2 pounds. World record white grunt is 6 pounds, 8 ounces. The tomtate is a commonly caught species that is used as live bait when hooked onto a king mackerel rig and cast over the side while anglers are bottom fishing.

Haywire Twist—A style of knot used in tying single-strand wire leaders consisting of wraps twisted around one another at an angle of less than 45 degrees. The haywire twist is usually finished with barrel wraps.

Hopkins Spoon—Trade name for a type of metal fishing lure (*Hopkins*, Norfolk, VA).

Jelly Ball—Jellyfish that look like balls of pink or purple jelly. The mantles are round in appearance and from about 6 to 10 inches in diameter. Jelly balls are preferred bait for spadefish. Also called cannonballs.

Jig—A lure that consists of a metal head with a hook and a dressing of natural hair (bucktail), artificial fibers, hard plastic strands (tinsel), or a soft plastic trailer that imitates shrimp or baitfish.

Kingfish—An angler's name for king mackerel.

Light Lining—Setting a live bait over the side without trolling, usually when the boat is drifting or anchored while bottom fishing.

Livewell—A tank that keeps bait alive by the intake and discharge of water through the use of a pump.

Loop Knot—A style of knot that passes through the eye of a lure or hook without cinching down tight. Loop knots allow free movement of a lure but sacrifice some line strength.

Loran-C—Loran-C was developed to provide radio-navigation for U.S. coastal waters and was later expanded to include coverage of the continental U.S. and Alaska, Canadian waters and the Bering Sea. It's a land-based system. Application of new receiver technology has allowed accuracy whereby users can return to within 50 meters of a previously determined position. Its status as a navigation aid is under review and it will be operated by the U.S. Government until it's no longer necessary or cost effective.

Mantle—The rounded, tough covering of the top of a jellyfish.

Megabait—Trade name used by the manufacturer of a style of metal fishing spoon that can be cast, trolled or jigged (*Pace Products, Inc.*, China).

Menhaden, Atlantic (*Brevoortia tyrannus*)—A baitfish with brassy sides, a dark bluish-green back and numerous spots on the side behind a dark shoulder spot that feeds by filtering plankton from seawater and congregates in large schools. Also called pogy, mossbunker, bunker, fatback.

Mullet, Popeye (*Mugil cephalus*)—An important forage fish and baitfish, popeye mullet are often seen leaping from the waters of estuaries and channels. Also called jumping mullet, black mullet, finger mullet, ball bat, striped mullet.

Naked—Angler term for a bait or lure fished without a dressing or teaser.

Outrigger—Long poles rigged on each side of an offshore fishing boat by which closed loops of line on pulley arrangements allow fishing lines to be trolled from release clips positioned out from the sides of the boat. The use of outriggers allows the trolling of more lines in a variety of positions than if the lines were set only from the gunwales and stern of the boat.

Peeler Crab—A blue crab that is beginning to shed its shell. Peeler crabs make good baits for some game fish.

Plane—Position of a boat hull when it's at a great enough speed to skim across the water surface, rather than plow through the water.

Planer—A metal or plastic device that takes a lure or bait down below the water surface by providing an angled profile with resistance against the direction of travel. A planer "trips" when a fish strikes or when an angler creates slack in the planer's line to expose its edge to the direction of travel and thereby decrease the resistance when the planer is retrieved.

Porgy (Jolthead–*Calamus bojanado*; Knobbed–*C. nodosus*; Red–*Pagrus pagrus*; Saucereye–*C. calomus*; Whitebone–*C. Leucosteus*; Spottail Pinfish–*Diplodus holbrooki*)—Porgies are often caught by anglers while fishing for grouper and snapper. Small species, like the spottail pinfish, commonly weigh less than a pound while the highly sought red porgy commonly weighs up to 6 pounds. Red porgy are subject to severe limits on recreational and commercial harvest. World record red porgy is 17 pounds.

Port—The left side of a boat as an angler faces the bow.

Pot—A wire mesh cage used to catch sea bass, crabs, lobsters, and other seafood.

Reef Ball—Trade name for a patented reef-building structure made of concrete with a hollow interior and holes in the walls to simulate natural coral formations.

Release Clip—A mechanical device that allows a fishing line to be suspended from an outrigger, downrigger, reel seat or stern. When a fish strikes, the line is released from the outrigger or downrigger line.

Ribbonfish (*Trichiurus lepturus*)—Ribbonfish have long, silvery bodies, a tapering, filamentous tail and sharp, arrow-shaped teeth. Ribbonfish make top baits for big king mackerel and can be caught with hook and line or bought in bait shops. Also called Atlantic cutlassfish.

Sabiki—A bait-catching rig consisting of a main line and three or more branch lines or droppers, each sporting a small hook usually having a gold finish and decorated with feathers, thin strips of processed fish skin, small plastic attractors and/or luminous beads. *Sabiki* rigs may also be called gold-hooks, quills or bait-maker rigs.

Sargassum—A type of seaweed that floats by means of gas bladders. Masses of Sargassum are important nurseries for multitudes of marine animals and attract game fish, especially dolphin.

Sea Witch—Trade name for a trolling skirt made of synthetic fibers with a metal band used ahead of a live or natural bait to give it motion and color (*Ultimate Tackle, Inc.* Jacksonville, FL).

Seven Strand Wire—Cable consisting of seven strands of wire cable, uncoated or coated with plastic, that is used as a leader material.

Shark, Atlantic Sharpnose (Rhizoprionodon terraenovae)—A small shark that is excellent eating with a snout that is longer than the mouth is wide. Dorsal and caudal fins are edged in black. Common weights are 2 to 10 pounds. World record is 16 pounds.

Shark, Blacktip (*Carcharhinus limbatus*)—A large shark with black tips on its dorsal and pectoral fins. Blacktips are good fighters. World record is 270 pounds, 9 ounces.

Shark, Dusky (C. obscurus)—A large grayish or brownish shark identified by a ridge between the dorsal fins. Dusky sharks are good fighters. World record is 764 pounds.

Shark, Great Hammerhead (*Sphyrna mokarran*)—A large shark that often exceeds 500 pounds with a head that has the eyes out on projections that make it resemble a sledgehammer when viewed from the top. There are also other species of hammerhead sharks, but the great hammerhead is the most common. World record is 991 pounds.

Shark, Sandbar (C. phumbeus)—A gray to brown, medium sized shark with wide, triangular dorsal and pectoral fins. The dorsal fin is situated almost directly above the pectoral fin, which distinguishes the sandbar shark from the dusky shark. The sandbar is a good fighter. Common weights are 50 to 100 pounds. World record is 260 pounds.

Shark, Tiger (*Galeocerdo cuvieri*)—The tiger is a large shark that is dark above and yellowish below with dark vertical lines or, in juveniles, rows of spots. The largest shark likely to be encountered by Carolina offshore anglers, many tigers weighing over 1,000 pounds have been landed. World record is 1,780 pounds. As with many of the large sharks, there are catch restrictions on tiger sharks to protect populations.

Shotgun—The longest line set in a trolling pattern, usually set from a T-top or the stern of a boat.

Shrimp Boat—A boat specifically designed to catch shrimp by trawling.

Silversides, Atlantic (*Menidia menidia and other Meindia sp.*)—A small, schooling fish of coastal waters, greenish above, pale below, usually with a prominent silver strip along the sides.

Silversides are important forage fish for Spanish mackerel and bonito.

Single Strand Wire—A type of wire leader material that consists of one strand, either stainless steel or titanium.

Smoker—Large king mackerel of over 30 pounds, so called because of the way they make water vapor evaporate from the reel at the speed of the strike (Carolina definition) or because they make the best eating when smoked on the grill (Florida definition).

Snake—A small king mackerel of up to 10 pounds, so called because of their thin appearance.

Snapper Bluefish—A small bluefish.

Snapper (Dog–*Lutjanus jocu*; Gray–*L. griseus*; Lane–*L. synagris*; Red–*L. campechanus*; Schoolmaster–*L. apodus*; Silk–*L. vivanus*; Vermillion–*Rhomboplites auronubens*)—These are the most likely species to be encountered by offshore anglers while bottom fishing. Snapper are good eating and the various species typically weigh from less than a pound for the Vermillion and Lane snapper to the highly sought red snapper which commonly weighs up to 10 pounds. World record red snapper is 50 pounds, 4 ounces.

Spadefish, Atlantic (*Chaetodipterus faber*)—Spadefish have vertical black stripes and a rounded body with a divided dorsal fin. Spadefish are edible and are caught by chumming with jelly balls above reefs. Common weights are 2 to 4 pounds. World record is 14 pounds.

Spanish Mackerel (*Scromberomorus maculatus*)—A mackerel with many gold spots on the side with a body that is proportionally deeper than a king mackerel. The lateral line tapers gently from front to back whereas the lateral line of a king mackerel takes a distinct dip. Also, the leading edge of the dorsal fin is dark. Common weights are 1 to 5 pounds. World record is 13 pounds.

Speck Rig—A terminal tackle rig consisting of two jigs tied to a single leader, also used for bluefish and other species.

Speckled Trout (*Cynoscion nebulosus*)—Many black spots and prominent canine teeth identify speckled trout, which has a dark gray to golden appearance. Common weights are 1 to 4 pounds. World record is 17 pounds, 7 ounces. More accurate common name is Spotted Seatrout.

Spiny Dogfish (*Squalus acanthias*)—A shark that is gray above, light gray below and has scattered light spots on the side. The second dorsal fin is smaller than the first dorsal fin and each has a sharp spike that can deliver a painful jab to an unwary offshore angler. This shark is excellent to eat. Common weights are 4 to 8 pounds. World record is 15 pounds, 12 ounces.

Spoon—A flattened or curved metal lure. Spoons of various designs are used for jigging, trolling and casting.

Spot (*Leiostomus xanthurus*)—The spot is a small fish that seldom reaches one pound in weight. The prominent black spot behind the gill plate is distinctive. Spots make good offshore baits for some game fish.

Sprat (Blueback Herring-*Alosa aestivalis*; Alewife–*A. pseudoharengus*)—Sprat is a term used by Carolina anglers to describe species of herring.

Squid (*Architeuthis sp.*)—A ten-armed mollusk with a slender conical body and broad tail flukes. Squid are important forage species and make good baits for many game fish.

Starboard—The right side of a boat as one faces the bow.

Stern—The rear of a boat.

Stingsilver—Trade name for a heavy meal lure that is usually jigged up and down to attract fish (*Haw River Tackle*, Burlington, NC).

Striped Bass (*Morone saxitilis*)—A silvery game fish that has seven to eight black horizontal stripes along the sides. Common weights are 5 to 20 pounds. World record is 78 pounds, 8 ounces. Also called linesider and rockfish.

Structure—offshore angler's term meaning any manmade or natural object projecting from the bottom or shoreline which attracts fish.

Superbraid—A type of fishing line that is braided from artificial fibers of modern design. Superbraids have more abrasion resistance and less stretch than Nylon braids.

Tailor Bluefish—Juvenile bluefish, so called because of the way they snip off plastic grub tails and live bait tails, leaving the jig or fish head intact and missing the hook.

Tarpon (*Megalops atlanticus*)—Tarpon are massive fish with large scales, silver sides, green back and dark, forked tail. A lone streamer runs off the rear of the dorsal fin. Tarpon are among the sportiest game fish, combining speed, aerial acrobatics and size. Common weights are 10 to 75 pounds. World record is 283 pounds, 4 ounces.

Tautog (*Tautoga onitis*)—A fish with a dark appearance and thick protruding lips (male) or more rounded head and mottled gray (female) with a single dorsal fin extending from above the pectoral fin to the beginning of the tail. Common weights are 2 to 5 pounds. World record is 25 pounds. Also called blackfish.

Tomtate —(See Grunt)

Triggerfish (Gray–*Balistes capriscus*; Queen–*B. vetula*; Ocean–*Canthidermis sufflamen*)—Triggerfish all have long dorsal spikes that lock into an erect position and can only be folded by pressing the "trigger," or the smallest spine to the rear of the dorsal fin. Common weights are 1 to 6 pounds. World record for the most common triggerfish, the gray triggerfish, is 13 pounds, 9 ounces.

Tripletail (*Lobotes surinamensis*)—A mottled brown fish with a deeply rounded shape, concave head and with the dorsal fin, anal fin and tail coming nearly together. Tripletail are uncommon in Carolina offshore waters, but are occasionally caught. Common weights are 2 to 12 pounds. World record is 42 pounds.

Trolling Skirt—A skirt or teaser made of hair, rubber or plastic that is tied ahead of a live or natural bait to add action and color.

T-top—An abbreviated top that is installed above a center console in offshore fishing boats. T-tops are made of canvas or fiberglass and help provide shade and protection from rain and sea spray as well as adding storage space for rods and instruments.

Tyger—Trade name for a brand of titanium wire used for leaders.

Mullet, Virginia (*Menticirrhus americanus*)—A small food fish with a long, light-colored body and chin barbell. These fish are fun to catch on light tackle and good to eat. Common weights are under 2 pounds. World record is 2 pounds, 5 ounces.

Weakfish (*Cynoscion regalis*)—A fish that is similar in appearance to a speckled trout except spots are very tiny and arranged in diagonal lines. Weakfish have prominent canine teeth and an overall gray appearance. Average weights are 2 to 4 pounds. World record is 19 pounds, 2 ounces. Also called gray trout.

Yo-Zuri—Trade name of a manufacturer of highly reflective plastic, minnow-imitating lures (*Yo-Zuri*, Tachibana, Takeo, Japan).

About the Author

Mike Marsh has written over 1,000 articles and newspaper columns about hunting and fishing for local and national publications. Many of those articles are about the hunting and fishing opportunities available in coastal North Carolina. His first book, *Carolina Hunting Adventures: Quest for the Limit*, was published by Atlantic Publishing, Tabor City, NC, in 1995 and is still in print.

His second book, *Inshore Angler: Coastal Carolina's Small Boat Fishing Guide*, published by Coastal Carolina Press in 2000, was intended as the first installment of a trilogy. *Offshore Angler: Carolina's Mackerel Boat Fishing Guide*, is intended as the predecessor to *Gulf Stream Angler*.

At the time *Offshore Angler* was published, Mike had served the sporting community for nine years as an outdoor columnist for the Wilmington *Star-News* and Tabor-Loris *Tribune*, and as the Southeastern Regional Editor of *Carolina Adventure* magazine, which became part of the Raleigh *News and Observer* Outdoor Section in 2003.

A prolific writer and photographer, he contributes outdoor-related news, articles, features and photographs to *North Carolina Game and Fish*, *North Carolina Sportsman*, *Wildlife in North Carolina*, *Tide*, *Striped Bass*, *Charlotte Observer* and many other regional and national publications. He has received numerous awards for his writing and photography skills from the Southeastern Outdoor Press Association (SEOPA) and the Outdoor Writers Association of America (OWAA).

Always an outdoorsman, he hunted and fished during his childhood and teenage years in the community of Climax, located in Guilford County, North Carolina. Upon earning an Associate in Applied Science (A.A.S.) degree in Fish and Wildlife Management from Wayne Community College in Goldsboro, N.C., he began working for the North Carolina Division of

Environmental Management in Mooresville, N.C. in 1973.

After living a hunting and fishing life on Lake Norman for 5 years, he moved to Wilmington in 1978 with his wife, Carol Elaine Jobe Marsh. Their son, Justin, was born in Wilmington in 1983. The family's hunting and fishing adventures have been the source for many of Mike's and Carol's articles.

Inshore Angler

Fishing/Sports/Outdoors
Price $16.00
Trade paper; 173 pages
Includes 38 photographs & 24 Maps
ISBN: 1-928556-21-3

Available at bookstores or from
Coastal Carolina Press
2231 Wrightsville Ave
Wilmington, NC 28403
877-817-9900 toll-free
910-362-9497 fax

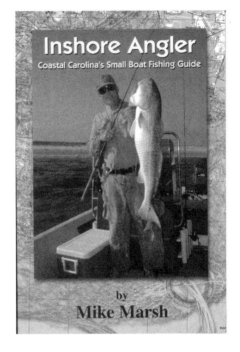

Inshore Angler is a collection of Marsh's most popular articles that tell anglers who own small john boats and skiffs how, when and where to catch the state's most highly prized saltwater inshore game fish such as flounder, red drum, bluefish, striped bass and black drum.

Many of the chapters are based on tips from the best inshore guides along the coast like Jimmy Price, David Mammay, and Tyler Stone. These guides stay booked far in advance at a price of hundreds of dollars per day. Now, their insights and experience can benefit anyone who has a few dollars to buy a book.